MW01286339

Business is **Decisions** **Success** is **Intuition**

Accelerate your Growth by
Improving Decision Making

Jephtah Lorch

Knowledge is power;
its application—an art.

to my wife and children with love

Table of Contents

Introduction

Life experience drives this book.

Through years of very intensive, mostly high-tech experience in creating sustainable change and growth, I have witnessed a multitude of situations, people, dreams, and disappointments in a multitude of environments and companies.

I have used willpower—mine and others'—to generate company drive and close the gap between reality and dream, existence and vision.

I have seen how simple matters are made complex and how complex matters are oversimplified.

I have observed egos, greed, fears, and misperceptions lead to unnecessary failure or unwarranted optimism.

I have experienced the loneliness of decision making, the pain of firing good family people.

I have known the sweetness of success and the bitterness of failure.

This book is about management, and how it can sow seeds of success or seeds of failure. It is also about the importance of qualitative goals and decision making and how to back them up with quantitative analysis and sanity checks. Over the next 14 chapters, I share the insights and lessons I have learned—both those I have learned from others and those I learned in my time as a turnaround CEO saving companies on the brink of failure.

Over the years, I have led companies to successful turnarounds and their subsequent sale. I have turned bankrupt companies into cash cows. I have identified material flaws in companies' business models and successfully repositioned them.

In one instance, the flaws were so critical that I led to a company's closure—a company that many perceived as a great investment. My reason? The basis on which people *thought* the company was a good investment was faulty; the company had been built on sand, not rock. Management had neglected to look at the full market food chain of which it was part, and so hadn't seen the oversupply that doomed the company. Three months after the company was closed, my analysis proved correct—the market collapsed.

It wasn't only the management that overlooked the oversupply problem; market forecasters did as well. I hadn't relied only on their conclusions; I analyzed their and other information and drew my own conclusions.

Ideally, the people who have access to all the information—such as CEOs—should be the ones making the decisions, and they should do so after carefully analyzing all their information, not only relying on other people's analyses.

In practice, things aren't that simple. People cling to comfort zones, to social pressures and expectations. We are prisoners of the professional and social webs to which our lives are attached and on which they depend. We fear stepping out of the "mechanics" of life and the inertial loops dictated by our pasts and by our environments.

And that's not the way to succeed.

To succeed, we need to form our own ideas and opinions and make independent decisions. We need to break out of our comfort zones. In both our personal and our professional lives, we need to base our decisions first and foremost on qualitative goals and visions—not only on quantifiable numbers. Ask questions like are we leading in the right direction? Numbers can't tell us, but our hearts and guts can. What numbers *can* tell us is whether the techniques we're using to go in a certain direction match up with the reality of, for example, funding.

In our personal lives, we must ask these questions for the sake of ourselves and our families. In our professional lives, we ask them on behalf of our companies.

There is no single management theory that applies to any company in the world. There is, however, one practical (and hopefully successful) management practice for each company: the leadership, thinking, and execution that the CEO and his or her executives instill.

This book shares experiences, qualitative concepts, and tools to simplify thinking and the execution of managerial tasks. While this book describes corporate dilemmas, its high-level concepts are applicable in all facets of our lives, including government, security, health, non-profit organizations, education, and our personal lives.

I've done my best to make this book clear and easy to read—and as simple as all things in business and life should be.

Jephtah Lorch
September, 2015

Chapter 1:
Back to Basics

What Is a Company?

In this section, we'll discuss both a) what a company is and b) the driving factors that help companies navigate long-term growth paths in normal times and survive rough waters in hard times.

Companies are special creatures. They have rights and obligations but not brains, souls, muscles, wishes, or even bodies. Despite this, they are alive, growing, and developing; and they have illnesses, successes, childhood, maturity, rebirth, and more.

In a sense, a company is like a child: it has a guardian family, is in an ongoing learning and improvement process, and may decide to change its profession.

Companies seek to grow and improve while living in a constantly changing environment. However, by themselves, companies are incapable of exercising and executing their rights and obligations.

It is here, in the nurturing of the company through qualitative decisions, that the seeds of success or failure are sown. Each company has to be treated and nurtured according to its personality, its goals, critical mass, strength, and needs. Larger corporations, which have muscle and possibly some fat, will need a different diet than smaller, lighter companies.

What then bridges the gap between the abstract concept of a company and the fact that it is alive? What bridges the gap between the intangible, immeasurable, yet crucial factors in the formation and life of a company and its reality?

People. People conceive companies, nurture them, grow them, and are passionate about them. People are the guardians, brains, hearts, souls, drives, eyes, ears, and muscles of companies. They are the ones caring for, protecting, educating, and feeding the brain children called companies.

All companies are based on and around and are dependent on people—their cultures, needs, work abilities, knowhow, personalities, and whims. A company's dependency on people makes it essential for managers to connect with and promote their company to all the people circles with which they and the company interact.

People are the ones who establish companies in order to fulfill a certain task or need. The need may already exist, or the company's management may seek to create it. The need may be real or perceived, but it always has to fulfill a client need.

People are the clients, the first and most important source of success and the people who primarily feed the company its main survival food—cash. If people do not consume products and services, the economy will collapse.

People are the company employees who manufacture, develop, and sell its products or services.

People are bankers, suppliers, subcontractors, designers, shareholders, and so on. It is these people, outside the company, who decide when, how much, and under what terms they'll give cash to the company.

Completing the Cycle

There is one central reason for which a business exists: to fulfill a need. I call the process of fulfilling this need the lifeblood cycle: 1) a product is developed, 2) it is manufactured, 3) it is sold, and 4) payment is collected.

Figure 1 - The Simplified Business Lifeblood Cycle

A good cycle is harmonized and synchronized by management and employees to ensure profitability and long-term sustainability. Success results from how well all corporate participants understand the full cycle and their contribution to its success—as measured in ongoing sales and profitability.

There is typically a learning gap in new startup companies and in companies or monopolistic organizations like government.

Startups are driven by great ideas and personal drives. During their initial development phases, before they have clients, startups are led by decisive people with dreams and ideas, people who are able to raise funding and control egos. It isn't until the first time a sale is made and client interactions come to life that a company's team realizes what real-world sales are about: clients. This can mean everything from client meetings, the need for product features, pricing, serviceability, quality, and stability issues to matters of taste such as colors, graphics, designs, and how the product is shipped. The reality that the client is the boss is further amplified when that client fails to pay, turning great expectations into bitter feelings of disappointment and failure.

An impressive success story is UK-based Virgin Group, established and led by the dyslexic gentleman Sir Richard Branson.

Sir Richard started out by completing the lifeblood cycle selling records, drawing people to buy his products and reinvesting in his company. A born entrepreneur, Sir Richard continued to his next venture, Virgin Air. Nowadays, after many other ventures, Sir Richard is pioneering commercial space flights with Virgin Galactic. How does he keep succeeding? Sir Richard understands i) people and their needs, ii) the need to complete the cycle—and, iii) he has the guts to break away from comfort zones.

Monopolistic and large hierarchical corporations often unknowingly or unintentionally distance employees from clients. Employees develop the notion that job security has to do with their relationships with superiors rather than their relationships with clients. They may be right when superiors and managers are busy with irrelevant factors like egos and control, but such attitudes are ruinous. Bringing employees and managers closer to clients and listening to client needs, complaints, and wishes will change a team's perception. Inspired by CEOs and top managements, client-oriented policies improve employees' understanding of why companies exist.

In a telecom equipment company I managed before the burst of the dot-com bubble, I found countless clients were confused by the many different types of new equipment, options, and advantages offered on the market.

My great development staff showed ingenuity, creativity, and clout; but I wanted them to also listen to clients, hear a voice, and see a face. I wanted them to get a firsthand feel for clients, their concerns and expectations, and to convince them, the clients, that our offering was the best choice. I therefore brought R&D managers to our booth at our next exhibition and had them spend a week talking to clients.

During that week, the R&D managers realized that clients are concerned not only with great technology, but also with very practical and mundane issues such as compatibility with other equipment, cost, reliability, and service. Client concerns suddenly had a face, a voice, and a personality. The experience positively changed the R&D team's perception and helped improve the company as a whole.

Management

The art of nurturing a company is called management. Management is first and foremost about the qualitative aspects of leading and running a company, including its philosophy and its intangible characteristics (such as integrity and corporate culture). It is about leadership in good and especially through hard times. It is about employee leadership, the energy of which will radiate to clients, suppliers, financiers, and beyond. It is about corporate culture, product lines, and today's decisions about which goals should be reached two to five years down the line and how.

The heart and soul of the company is the CEO. The CEO makes the lifeblood flow. He or she ensures that the brain gets enough oxygen, balances body and mind, nurtures muscles, and ensures learning. Company employees contribute muscle and sensory organs like eyes, ears, and fingers. They are the brains and limbs, the kinetic energy of the company. Employees fulfill functions like research and development, sales and marketing, product marketing, client support, manufacturing, administration, and other corporate functions. The drive and heart behind them is the CEO.

The CEO is also the chief strategist, leader, and spokesperson. He or she spearheads corporate strategy and sees to it that the body of the company is properly fed. As spokesperson, the CEO is also the chief salesperson. His or her personality, integrity, vision, and execution abilities are crucial to gaining public and employee support and recognition. Shareholders and their board of directors will support and promote the company (or not) because of its CEO. Shareholder trust in the company's management also attracts the trust of suppliers, bankers, and clients. People follow promising and successful leadership.

Company Activities

Companies have four key corporate activities or limbs: Sales & Marketing, Research & Development, Finances, and Operations (Figure 2, below).

Take a look at the figure. The top two boxes represent the root cause of a company's existence, its reason for being. They are a company's revenue generator—the top line of a company's financial statements. The two bottom boxes represent the support activities that affect a company's profit or loss—the bottom line.

Figure 2 - A Company's Four Limbs

All four limbs must be proportionately strong, complementing and balancing each other. A strong R&D group paired with a poor sales group will lead to failure; similarly, acceptance of a large purchase order without manufacturing facilities or working capital to finance such a purchase order would be disastrous. Head and body must be synchronized. And in order to achieve this, the CEO must instill positive, supportive, and cooperative energies in his or her employees.

Qualitative and Quantitative Decisions

Another important aspect of any company is the sort of decision making that goes on, consciously or unconsciously. There are two basic types of decisions: qualitative and quantitative.

Qualitative decisions are decisions based on gut feelings—which is to say, the intuitive integration of our intellect, life experience, knowhow, emotions, and so on. Qualitative decisions cannot be quantified unless simplified and reduced for quantification purposes (although the choice of simplification tools is still qualitative). If the decision maker has a better feeling about B than about A, B wins—even if the numbers support A.

Examples: "This business plan shows great profits, but my gut feeling tells me the market is shifting elsewhere," or "I decided not to buy this house because it just didn't seem nice enough. Also, I didn't like the color."

One last thing: emotions can impact decisions. Understanding this—and understanding which emotions are driving you—can help you avoid making decisions you'll later regret. The opposite is also true: we may have a bad gut feeling about doing business with someone, yet the business opportunity seems tempting, and thus we go ahead with it.

Quantitative decisions are decisions based on solid facts and numbers. They are not based on gut feelings or intuition. Our quantitative decisions are measurable in a variety of terms like money, size, color, or weight. If the numbers say A is bigger than B, A wins—even if the decision-maker has a bad feeling about B.

Example: "I decided not to buy this house because I didn't have enough money to afford it."

Of course, in most cases, a combination of qualitative and quantitative reasoning is used. No one is going to buy a house they dislike just because they can afford it, and most people will think twice about buying a house they like but can't afford.

Out-of-the-Box Thinking

Thinking is the conscious use of our brains to put together and analyze information. The *box* represents the database from which our brain is accustomed to working. When you think out of the box, you are seeking to (a) expand the database and (b) handle your thoughts from a new perspective, one outside your typical thinking or comparison conventions. To do this, you have to consciously and simultaneously handle two threads: the data (what you're thinking about) and the process (how you're thinking).

Thinking is essential. This may seem obvious, but the truth is that adults tend to replace thinking with habit. Our mental reflex is to compare situations with past mental recollections of similar experiences—which, in many cases, leads us to mistaken choices or answers. Habit is helpful, but it can't replace thinking.

Basing decisions on careful thought and a wider data base rather than habitual response helps managers assess trends, clients, and the general economic situation and relate daily activities to their markets. It helps them break away from comfort zones and mechanical, standardized, me to thought patterns.

Analysis and conclusion-drawing are mental sports. They help us solve logic problems, sharpen our ability to identify crucial details, and so on.

Most of us have taken logic tests at one time or another, such as those in the GMAT. Some of us took courses teaching us tricks to help with these problems. In fact, what we were learning wasn't tricks but new thinking patterns— or, rather, *what for us* were new thinking patterns. Such preparation courses help us break away from the comfort-zone thinking patterns that lead to mental stagnation.

To put it another way: we need to get reaccustomed to thinking instead of comparing things with past recollections.

We should also enrich our box by learning new things. This is important; if we don't learn new things, we'll be basing our decisions on comfortable but outdated information. The world is dynamic and rich with news and novelties. Certain news items are relevant; others are not. Our data collection and analysis efforts have to be based on the current relevance of each piece of information. For example, if we operate in the United States and there is a monetary crunch in Europe, we should ask ourselves if and how such a crunch can affect our business. We should not write off the crunch because it is in Europe.

Out-of-the-box thinking means breaking comfort zone patterns and increasing our radiuses and depths of learning and thinking. Life is about self-improvement. The opportunities are there, but it is up to us to reach out and make them happen.

Plan and Execute: From Strategy to Tactics

Before we go further, I'd like to give you a couple of definitions:

Strategy is a military word meaning "a plan of action designed to achieve a particular goal" and is concerned with how different engagements or battles are linked to reaching that goal. Whether a battle should be fought at all is a matter of strategy.

Tactics is the conduct of an engagement. Tactics is how a battle is fought, and considers things like terrain, enemy forces, weather, and resources.

We can generalize by stating that strategy is the *what* while tactics are the *how*.

Good choices of strategy and tactics are both necessary to grow healthy companies or save distressed ones.

For distressed companies, time is of the essence. While money bleeding is a daily constant, infusion of funds through investment or sales is not feasible or is too small. Progress must be shown each and every day, small or big. Management turnaround efforts must be led like a battle in motion, hitting the ground running, assuming new surprises and obstacles at any given time. Initially, this battle is a reactive one with little room for initiative. It is an attempt to hold ground with minimal retreat. As the company stabilizes, management can take action by improving efficiency, regaining client trust, introducing new products, improving service, revising pricing and costs, selling inventories, and implementing other cash-generating activities. Daily tactical efforts are patiently led to converge with the new strategy. The priorities are the same as when drowning: first regain breath, and then start looking for safe haven or shore. We start out with a reactive attitude and, with the improving situation, shift to proactive behavior.

Strategies need to be clear and formulated in simple, comprehensible, and executable terms. The first step is to announce a qualitative direction for a baseline. In Sememe[1] (see Chapter 2), I set two such goals: 1) focus on sales via small resellers, and 2) reduce manufacturing costs through product redesign. The first goal I implemented immediately; the second took time especially because of lacking resources.

Over time, strategy should be adjusted, corrected, further refined, or improved. Quantification is used to verify progress and provide sanity checks. It is used in parallel to high-level qualitative sanity checks (see Chapter 3).

The reality of distressed companies forces them to initially plan for a few realistic, lower-risk actions and immediate goals. Whereas rich companies can afford to target multi-tier or multi-pronged strategies where some goals are not met while others succeed, compensating for losses caused by the former.

Internal Logic

One of the CEO's first duties is to analyze the company strategy to make sure it is coherent and has sound internal logic. "Internal logic," in this case, means that the strategy reasonably incorporates and works for all four of the company's limbs: Research & Development, Sales & Marketing, Operations, and Finances.

Before I joined Sememe, a company I turned around, internal logic was definitely missing.

Sememe's chairman, despite negative assets on Sememe's balance sheet and having no free cash, decided to acquire its foreclosed competitor in order to, hopefully, gain market share. No one asked why management thought that it could improve a bankrupt company when

---

1   Alias for a company I turned around.

its own company was being mismanaged into bankruptcy. No one asked how financing a bankrupt, old-technology company with almost no sales was cheaper than investing in Sememe's own sales force (see Chapter 8 on Delegation of Incompetence). It wasn't long before Sememe had to close the acquired company.

The Human Factor

In distressed companies, the human factor is a crucial anchor for any turnaround strategy. Funding cannot replace the humans who sell, buy, communicate, share ideas, open markets, develop products, trade wares, and consume. In general, it is we—humans—who make things happen.

Management should apply strategies in ways that nurture teamwork and enhance motivation—which will lead to improved efficiency, better use of resources, and improved effectiveness. The human factor contribution is further amplified when continuous and constant change is required. To achieve such change, dedicated and proactive people should be in place. Distressed companies do not have time or funding to hire expensive, high-flying managers or adopt complex IT systems.

Chapter 2:
Saving Sememe

This chapter could also be called *Thriving on Chaos*. More than anything, this book was inspired by my encounter with an amazing company full of highly intelligent, intellectually capable yet managerially incompetent people whose academic degrees failed to compensate for their lack of people, system overview, and leadership skills. Combined with a healthy level of greed, the company's saga wouldn't have been out of place in a soap opera.

To make things easy, let's call the company Sememe. Sememe was a seven-year-old optical wireless company, and it had reached the verge of bankruptcy. It was financially over-leveraged and had negative assets on its balance sheet. Sales were negligible and business goals unreached. Investors had lost faith in its management and interest in the company. Furthermore, Sememe had lately acquired a financially distressed competitor—a move that only increased management pressures.

Sememe's founder was a very charismatic person, but he was unable to run a company. He'd succeeded in raising funds from twenty-two shareholders, private and institutional, before they'd stopped believing him and in him. Under pressure from the institutional shareholders, he was forced to bring professional management on board. That's how I found myself there as a consultant-turned-CEO.

I spent nearly three years working at Sememe. By the time I left, we were able to sell the company for over seven times the funds invested in it. Not bad for a company previously on the verge of bankruptcy!

Before I came to Sememe, there were other consultants. They went in, presented their reports, and left. Nothing improved.

As time went by, cash dwindled, creditor pressure increased, motivation fell, and the company slowed down. That was when I was called in.

Because of the tight cash situation, I carried out a one-week, high-level analysis; and, unlike the other consultants, I delivered a two-page report, which surprised the chairman, who was used to long reports. My report pointed to the basic, high-level problems rather than lower-level and execution-related flaws—I concentrated on the cause, not the symptoms, of the disease.

I kept my recommendations short because of reader filters—that is, because details may be differently understood or misunderstood due to different reader and writer life experiences. Such time-consuming misunderstandings are prohibitive when cash is scarce.

My most important conclusions were that what Sememe was offering had a) good core technology, b) differentiators (i.e. elements that made it unique; the products or services it offered were not indistinguishable from its competitors'), and c) market appeal.

Sememe was therefore potentially valid as a company. Its problems were due to poor execution of its activities—namely, its top-line sales and bottom-line activities. These elements were mismanaged, if they were managed at all. This important conclusion was the basis for my staying and continuing to the next stage.

The next issue was leadership. The dominant person in the company was the chairman, who was also the controlling shareholder. He was incapable of managing the company. Existing management had no suitable candidates for the CEO's position, not even the acting CEO, because there was no one willing to challenge the chairman or stand up to him. This situation is a typical people's deadlock—that is, a situation in which a damaging status quo is established and maintained.

After I presented and explained my report to the chairman and board, the chairman asked me to stay on and take charge of the improvements. He was desperate. I asked him: "Will you run the company with me as your advisor?"

"You implement the changes," he replied.

I made it clear that in that case, to avoid confusion and conflicting messages, there had to be one CEO. By hiring me to implement the changes, he would effectively be replacing the acting CEO—who had been against bringing in a consultant in the first place.

The chairman said, "You will be the CEO." The CEO resigned, and I stayed on to implement the methods described in this book.

Like many chaotic situations, the blame game was on, as were politics and stressed personal relations. I drew the heat to myself in a successful attempt to isolate management from negative energies and help them focus on their newly defined immediate tasks—thus avoiding unnecessary friction.

The positive shift had begun.

Sales

In Sememe, company sales depended on sales managers who lacked motivation or ability. Sales managers had trouble generating sales leads and identifying and developing new clients and distributors.

Since there was no extra money to work with, I recruited all the company's secretaries to work as back office sales agents, making each responsible for a geographical sales area. Each received a potential distributor and client database, and guidelines on how and where to find additional databases. Each received their sales process, sales kit information, and instructions to get more distributors and clients on board.

The result? Mass exposure and a domino effect. We reached potential clients with real names and telephones, and we did it in such a way that we were talked about in markets and professional circles.

This mass exposure created leads and sales. The company boomed into public awareness, and our sales representatives began competing for local representation and distribution. Our sales managers then focused on closing deals rather than generating leads or waiting for clients to call.

The people in the expanding sales network were not aware of the company's poor financial situation; they judged the company on its offering, message, and the energies and persistence of its team. They liked what they saw. The results of the new sales techniques were fantastic to the point that sales growth was limited only by the manufacturing budget!

Creativity was always used. After stabilizing the company, we began participating in international exhibitions like CeBIT, an eight-day industrial exhibition in Germany. CeBIT published a daily newspaper in which I wanted exposure. I approached its editor, who said that the paper covered technologies, not specific companies, and proposed that I find a competitor to appear with us. Well, I did. I brought a representative of one of Japan's top five electronic companies, which had a similar offering. The next day, an article was published, its picture showing Japan's top company and bankrupt Sememe as equals.

Service

The next problem Sememe faced was service. When there were issues in Sememe's previously installed systems, clients and distributors became frustrated—and more frustrated still when Sememe was unable or unwilling to fix those issues. This led distributors to abandon Sememe, causing material loss of clients and sales.

The solution was simple although initially expensive: we addressed every issue current customers had worldwide. Solutions were provided regardless of cost. This entailed, in some cases, sending new equipment to replace problematic units.

Although doing that was expensive, the message it sent was concise and powerful: we would support our business partners and clients no matter what.

The message worked. Distributors and representatives accelerated their efforts, and order intake increased threefold. A small home-office-based representative in New Zealand grew his sales eightfold!

Products

Sememe's core technology was good, and it had strong differentiators and market appeal. Its biggest problem was the products' gross margin.

Gross margin is worked out like this:

$$Gross\ Margin\ (\%) = \frac{revenue - cost\ of\ goods\ sold}{revenue}$$

At that time, companies in the same industry could expect a respectable 40% gross margin. Sememe's gross margin was only 15%. The company could not survive without going through a comprehensive development and manufacturing improvement program to reduce costs.

Remember what I said about qualitative vs. quantitative thinking in Chapter 1? Here's an example: previous managements' *qualitative* understanding was that Sememe was spending too much compared to how much it was making. Their quantitative analyses were mistaken, so they could not identify the problem. That's what caused the losses. Our *quantitative* goal was to raise Sememe's gross margin from 15% to at least 40%. With these things in mind, a new and quantifiable master goal was defined for both R&D and manufacturing divisions, targeting two key factors:

- Cost reduction to be achieved by a full product line redesign, which would reduce the cost of both materials and manufacturing.

- During the same process, I also asked to expand the product line. To this end, I gave specific guidelines that targeted untapped market opportunities.

Achieving these goals required a thorough redesign of Sememe's full product line and manufacturing processes. Quantitative goals were set. They included lowering total manufacturing costs, minimizing the number of parts in each product, maximizing the number of common parts in all products, minimizing the number of parts handled in inventory, reducing assembly and testing hours, and expanding the product line.

To go about this, I defined goals. As you read these goals, note that most of them stem from qualitatively thinking about the big picture. Execution requires quantification, but only quantification of the *right* strategy. Our goals were as follows:

- Create a unified platform for all products. This platform should add and expand product performance.

- Replace limited-life-expectancy parts (like lasers) with long-life-expectancy devices.

- Reduce assembly, testing, and tuning time by 50%. This could be done by increasing automation, improving product software, reducing mechanical assembly time, unifying mechanical parts, and lowering the number of bolts and screws.[2]

- Reduce the number of subcontractors, suppliers, and components.

- Move to annual and multi-year purchasing plans with optional delivery changes.

---

2   I learned this from an article I read early on in my career about the SONY Walkman. Sony redesigned the Walkman to reduce cost. The post-redesign analysis showed that the reduction of the number of assembly screws was a major cost saver because it reduced manual labor.

The master-plan proved very successful. Inventories were drastically reduced; assembly and tuning times were cut by almost 50%, saving expensive manpower; and the new extended-range units were unique on the market, achieving a 70% gross margin!

In short: with this new product line, we boosted sales and made the company profitable.

Finances

Sememe's finances were a mess. The books showed profits when there were actually great losses, no financial facilities like bank credits were available, and debts exceeded assets. The old management had renegotiated huge debts only to fail to comply with the new terms, and creditors had lost patience. Checks were written and stashed in a drawer but registered as if they were cashed. Suppliers called daily, and banks halted credit lines.

In simple terms, there were three main problems:

- Chaos in the books and no financial visibility
- Debts to important suppliers and creditors
- Lack of working capital

Here's how we dealt with them.

Chaos in the Books

I started by stabilizing cash flow. My later goals were showing profit in the Profit & Loss (P&L) statement and then restructuring the Balance Sheet.

We set up a new cash flow management tool that looked into the future and considered every possible expense, including past debts. This gave me expense-side visibility.

Debts to Important Suppliers and Creditors

We prioritized Sememe's expenses into must, nice to have, and useless payments. We focused on paying only for what was absolutely needed for the company's survival. We dealt with each type as follows:

Debts to much-needed suppliers on whom we depended. With this group, we negotiated debt repayment as part of a package deal that included reduced prices, long-term purchasing commitment, and partial debt repayment with each payment for new product delivery. Thus, as business grew, debt repayment was accelerated—which was win-win for Sememe and suppliers.

Debts to suppliers whose support was needed for long-term progress. We asked this group to wait patiently for the new management work to generate much-needed cash. Since lawsuits are costly and not necessarily beneficial, these suppliers, seeing the new attitude, waited patiently.

Suppliers with whom no further business was foreseen. We delayed repaying debt to this group until we could negotiate debt discounts on cash payments down to 16 cents on the dollar.

A parallel effort was made to pay off all small amounts, as these were not worthy of management attention. One side benefit of this approach was that many of the small-sum suppliers, some of them large companies, liked the new management's approach and sought to increase their business with the company.

Lack of Working Capital

Last was the problem of lack of working capital (i.e. credit lines). We solved this in a number of ways:

To overcome the lack of banking credit facilities, we a) shifted our much-needed credit from banks and investors to supplier credit lines and b) accelerated cash turnaround on sales.

To lower cash usage, we consumed inventories, increased productivity, reduced manpower, and accelerated sales.

To reduce working capital need:

- Inventory was turned around more times per year—that is, we used and replenished inventory more quickly. This was made more possible by sales growth of the new lower cost and common parts product line.

- The new product lines provided higher gross margins and thus required less operating cash.

- We earmarked the freed-up cash for increasing sales, further accelerate manufacturing, and lower unit cost.

Payments were made twice a month to essential suppliers only (rather than to whoever nagged the most), reducing pressures and establishing structure and priorities.

A simple spreadsheet was used to tightly control cash flow and payments, and a tedious project was initiated to put order in the company's accounting books. The Chief Financial Officer was respectfully released from his job.

Accounting was instructed to tell creditors the truth about the company's situation. Previous corporate culture had been off track to the point that a bookkeeper once approached me to say, "I never knew I could tell the truth." Before, she had been consistently instructed to fend off creditors with excuses such as "The check is in the mail," "Tomorrow we will receive money," and "I promise you next week!"

If a supplier wanted to talk to the CEO, staff members were instructed to transfer the call. Suppliers were much happier to confront the top authority and accept clear and honest answers than the evasive and not necessarily true answers they'd previously received. Before long, far fewer creditors were calling. Debts were slowly reduced and, moreover, not a single lawsuit was filed against the company.

Within six months, cash bleeding was stopped and the cash-flow deficit began decreasing. After an additional year, positive cash-flow on operations (excluding debt repayment) was attained. Debt repayment, especially long-term debt, was still a burden, as was the lack of banking credit lines. A few months later, the P&L statement showed profit. It was time to put the balance sheet in order.

Creative Premises

Sememe was located in an industrial zone turned shopping and recreation center. It was far from airports and main roads and therefore had fewer interested and overseas visitors. The company needed to leave the old and rundown location to get closer to key highways, be in a high-tech area, improve the working environment, and send a message of positive change to clients, business partners, and employees. Unfortunately, the company's financial state made the move prohibitive.

Soon after I joined, a real estate agent who'd courted the previous management for over a year called, offering me alternative premises. My response was: "Give me six months to see if I have a company for the premises you offer."

The agent was patient and called back after six months. We met. During the meeting, I shared the company's financial situation with him. I showed him that cash bleeding had stopped and sales increased, but that the company was heavily in debt. "If you want us as a tenant, let me know," I told him.

To my surprise, the realtor called me the next day with a positive answer from the CEO of a company owning several possible buildings. After site visits, area calculations, and various discussions, we agreed on a location and started negotiating the terms and contract. When we reached the clause related to securities and collaterals, I reminded him of our company financials. "What can you offer instead?" he asked. "Options and warrants" was my answer. Here again, to my surprise, the landlord agreed. The deal was concluded.

Three years later, when the company was profitably sold, the holding company that owned the building exercised its options and was generously compensated for the risk it took in accepting a financially troubled tenant.

A year or so after we moved into the new building, the realtor visited us. Over a cup of coffee, I mentioned that I was curious why the management of the holding company had agreed to take on such a huge risk. His response surprised me: "Tenants looking to rent space and buildings tell us about how successful they are and how much more money they will make. However, when it comes to actual rent payments, they ask for extensions and drift into pretexts. And here was someone who was transparent from day one."

In a few cases, I had to defer rent payments because of projected cash flow dips. With a reasonable notice, I asked the holding company to defer rent payments, which they always did. And they always got paid.

Investments and Investors

Prior to my joining the company, the chairman focused on solving symptoms rather than problems. The most notable symptom he concentrated on was lack of cash. Being charismatic, he managed to convince private and institutional investors to invest. However, as time went by, institutional investors lost interest in the company, private investments became smaller, and investment agreements became wrongfully shorter. The pressure led the chairman to sign agreements conflicting with the company's bylaws and previous investment agreements.

To deal with this, as the company improved, I led intensive diplomatic negotiations with the shareholders, and we established a new capitalization [shareholding] table. Thanks to the goodwill of the investors, we were able to save all their investments, and they reaped the rewards when the company was sold.

Corporate Culture

Corporate culture means the behavior, conduct, attitudes, beliefs, practices, communications, and ethics of a company. In Sememe, a drastic change was required.

Instead of paper memos, communications became verbal.

Instead of fearing the boss, employees shared problems with him or her and sought solutions *together*.

Instead of waiting for instructions, employees were permitted to use their initiative.

Instead of making long and tedious to-do lists, employees worked on three prioritized tasks.

It worked. People stopped reporting via long written reports, stopped wasting time on memos and filing. Desks were cleared. Time was freed for work, and that work brought results.

Managers broke down tasks into manageable blocks, supported their teams, verified execution, and received my backing as CEO when mistakes were made—even costly ones. That was only fair, because we all make mistakes, even good managers, and firing and hiring someone else is far more risky and costly.

Staff members unable or unwilling to join the momentum were let go, including the chairman's wife. This wasn't about power; it was an essential step to focus management, increase efficiency, and cut costs. As small successes were created and results became apparent, managers and teams became more enthusiastic, further accelerating their activities.

Value Creation

In three years, the company was harmonized, its internal logic aligned, its sales and profits increased, its debts paid, and its cash-flow problems solved. It had a healthy P&L and a strengthened balance sheet. All this resulted in the very profitable sale of the company.

An amazing end to a company most shareholders had written off.

Chapter 3:
From Vision to Strategy

The Importance of Qualitative Thinking

Improving companies, distressed or not, begins with qualitative thinking, with ideas and visions. Only once a vision exists, a strategy is fleshed out and executed using tactical measures.

In theory, the process of applying qualitative thinking and analysis is simple: one must simply do what one perceives will have the best outcome. The challenging part is implementation. Success depends on the people leading, the people involved, and the quality of thinking and spans of the horizons of both.

While there are certain standard models, I see the following four elements as necessary for success:

High-level goal: The company's vision.
Qualitative: In which direction should our company move?

Grand strategy: What needs to be achieved to make the vision into a reality. These sub-goals change and adapt with progress and time.
Qualitative: choice of executable goals.

Execution strategy: Strategic choice of means required to execute the grand strategy.
Qualitative: choice of execution tools and platforms.

Tactical execution: The use of the quantitative means, derived from qualitative ideas, to implement the execution strategy.
Quantitative: measurable execution.

For most people, the fine line between vision, grand strategy, execution strategy, and tactical activities is blurred.[3] Sharpening the lines and their roles in decision making helps break big decisions down to their smaller components, making them easier to deal with individually and as part of a process. In this section, therefore, I'll break down each step for you.

The Tipping Point

Before I move on, I'd like to take a moment to discuss the "tipping point." A well-structured qualitative decision seeks a balance—the tipping point—between the most important long-term growth factors. It considers, for example, issues like flexibility, adaptability, economies of scale, and barriers to entry.

High capital expenditure in a mass-manufacturing facility demands high investments but will be less flexible, sometimes resulting in smaller long-term returns. The high investment and lack of flexibility represent an abrupt tipping point. A softer tipping point allows for growth combined with certain levels of flexibility but sacrifices mass manufacturing capabilities and lower costs.

Here are a couple of examples:

---

3   Partially because for many, strategy includes both grand strategy and execution strategy.

Abrupt tipping point: Investing in steel mills takes a huge investment of time and money. It is hard to generate alternative uses for the equipment and staff of a steel mill if the investment turns out to be uneconomic.

Softer tipping point: Many high-technology and software companies show great flexibility and agility by outsourcing non-core activities, which allows them to make relatively quick corrections to adapt to changing market needs.

As executives and decision makers, we strive to develop plans with optimal (for the company) tipping point transitions to retain flexibility within industry limits.

Tipping point(s) should be kept in mind when planning the four steps: vision, grand strategy, execution strategy, and tactical execution.

The High-Level Goal or Vision

A company's high-level goal or vision defines its reason for existence, its contribution to society. The vision defines a dream, a need to be fulfilled through innovation, improvement, and so on.

The choice of vision is critical, and although it can easily be corrected before its implementation, once a vision is implemented, it is very hard and costly to change.

Sticking by a good vision will make a company tolerant to corrections in execution mistakes. In order to develop a healthy vision, one must understand what qualitative thinking and qualitative decision making are.

Let us choose a nutraceuticals company as an example. The company's high-level goal may be:

- Our company will *produce* nutraceuticals made of sea minerals and weeds, OR

- Our company will *become a significant player* in the production of nutraceuticals made of sea minerals and weeds, OR

- Our company will *be the market leader* in the production of nutraceuticals made of sea minerals and weeds.

All three statements deal with the same product and same market, but each statement represents a different ambition: production, significant market participation, or market leadership. Each ambition requires a different grand strategy.

Grand Strategy

The grand strategy is where success-creating advantages are clarified. The grand strategy will change with time to adapt the company or project to changing environments, economies, geopolitics, and so on.

Here are a few examples of grand strategies.

Over the next three to five years, our nutraceuticals company will:

- Focus on nutraceuticals based *only* on sea weeds and minerals.

- Use primarily sea components.

- Focus on weight-loss nutraceuticals.

- Focus on nutraceuticals consumed by the US market.

Each of these strategies has a different financial, operative, sales, and product development impact. Each possible strategy has to be qualitatively analyzed to make sure it fits with the high-level goal and to assess convergence and boundary problems. (We'll discuss convergence and boundary problems in Chapter 4.)

In our case, convergence analyzes sustainability, profitability over time, and ROI. Convergence also deals with questions like "When we succeed, will our competition imitate us, and, if so, how long will it take them to introduce a competitive product?"

The concept of boundary problems touches upon issues that crop up during transitions, such as making large investments, starting a business, developing new products, and development of new sales networks.

Ideally, project leaders should consider as many variables as they can reasonably deal with in order to make decisions. There are no magic recipes for designing a grand strategy, but there are some rules:

- Remain within the boundaries of the high-level goal.

- Exercise proactive, out-of-the-box thinking.

- Include only variables relevant to grand strategy and a little beyond.

- Know your risks and compromise knowingly.

- Say NO when necessary.

If strategy development reveals a major flaw in the high-level goal, then go back and review both.

In order to detect whether the company is drifting from its goals, check intermediate results against the previous step *and* the vision. The problem may have resulted from drifting slightly from the previous step, or it may be an accumulated drift stemming from the vision.

Execution Strategy

Execution strategy defines *how* we will execute the grand strategy.

Our nutraceutical company may decide to:

- Subcontract raw material processing, mixing, and packing.

- Have a fully self-sufficient manufacturing plant to reduce operating costs, increase flexibility, or protect trade secrets. Higher sales are required to justify such investment.

- Brand-label third party products in order to present a wider product variety.

All three are viable options, and all three *could* work with any of our high-level goals and grand strategies. The question is which will work best for the company, its strengths, and its leadership.

Here are a few points to consider when developing your execution strategy:

- The chosen execution strategy should be the most cost-effective and sustainable solution that fits with the grand strategy and the vision. "Thinking small," for example, impedes future growth.

- Execution strategy has to ensure the solution is within financial frameworks, market standards, manufacturing cycles, raw material seasonality, and so on.

- Complementary needs should also be considered, such as confidentiality in military-related industries, sterilization in medical consumables, and low cost in chewing gum stickers.

- Developing execution strategies should have soft enough tipping points to allow flexibility.

- Open minds, intellectual daring, and systematic work combined with street smarts lead to better decisions.

Tactical Execution

Tactical execution activities are the quantifiable steps that create and sell a product. It is at this stage that we work intensively using known design tools, project planning software, time/cost/output measurements, purchasing, and so on. This step is all about the details, technical or otherwise. Tactical execution flow is defined by the choice of the execution strategy.

If a crucial detail does not fall in place, revert to the execution strategy and upwards to see where tactical execution diverges from its qualitative goals.

While the three previous steps entail dreaming, thinking, and planning, tactical execution is all about the mechanics of a company. Tactical execution receives the most daily attention, consumes vast energies on a daily basis. The prior steps are far smaller consumers of time and daily attention, which means you must surpass yourself in order to shift your attention to the big picture and ask if it is still valid and working.

Tangible business aspects are mostly quantifiable and easier to assess and correct than qualitative aspects—which means that quantified activities can create a comfort zone. But it is the qualitative aspects, the high-level thinking and planning that determine a company's success or doom.

Sanity Checks

Once this initial work is done, but before implementation, it's time for a sanity check. This includes exploring asymptotes and convergence points and managing the boundary challenges, as we'll discuss in the next chapter.

It's easy to enslave yourself to the quantitative aspects of a business while forgetting about the qualitative aspects. For example, we never reach $1,000 in sales if the whole market is $1,000 and we have competition. For another thing, quantitative numbers might be based on false qualitative assumptions. Sanity checks can help you avoid such pitfalls that reflect, for example, a contradiction between qualitative goals and quantitative execution.

A sanity check is another name for a qualitative verification. A sanity check is done by revising the ideas behind the (tactical) numbers and by thinking about their strategic viability and sensitivity over time—when new technologies appear, with changing fashions, in different countries and cultures, and so on.

Sanity checks require very wide thinking radiuses— not unlike treasure hunts or quizzes.

Conclusion

The concept of applying qualitative thinking is simple; the implementation is complex. One needs to transcend technical details—identifying the critical ones and comparing them with the big picture. As no machine can run sanity checks, the sanity checks in a company will be as good as the person leading, defining the questions to be asked, and assessing the answers.

The effort qualitative thinking takes is negligible compared to the success or failure of a company. Start one step at a time, and you can turn your company around.

Never take any step for granted, and ensure you are out of your comfort and pre-programmed zones when making the sanity check.

The first step: challenge your mind and take a good look at what goes where.

Chapter 4:
Boundaries and Convergences

In the late 17th century, physicists Sir Isaac Newton and Gottfried Leibniz decided they needed a way to mathematically model physical phenomena in order to predict their outcome in space, over time or in a specific moment. Their models include paths of motion, effect of forces, electromagnetism, and so on.

Newton and Leibniz's work pioneered a new branch of mathematics called infinitesimal calculus. In management, we inadvertently use two of its tools: convergence and the boundary problem.

Convergence at the Extremes and the Boundary Problem

Let's start with a couple of simple definitions and examples.

Convergence at the Extremes

Convergence at the extremes deals with trends.

Let's say you're 50 years old and want to know what your monthly retirement payment will be when you retire at 65. In order to do so, you need to know two numbers: 1) your projected monthly contribution to your pension fund until retirement (assuming they'll stay the same), and 2) how many months are left until you retire.

Where these numbers (# of months and $/month) *converge* is called the *extreme*. In this example, the extreme is at retirement.

Of course, if you are making these calculations when you're only 50, the end number you get probably won't be perfectly accurate. For all you know, you might start making more money and be able to put more aside—or you might decide to retire earlier or later. Nevertheless, as long as things stay approximately the same, using the convergence at the extremes technique gives you a pretty good estimate of your retirement income.

Convergence can be used many different ways. For example, if you are given directions and begin driving, the extreme is the address you need to reach, and convergence is achieved by following the directions, which get you closer and closer as you follow them.

Convergence in business touches upon many aspects like trends in pricing, in technology, or in obtaining market share.

Boundary Problems

Boundary problems deal with the interface between two adjacent elements, activities, events, and so on.

Think of commercial airplanes. Most of the time, an airplane is in one of two states—flying at cruising altitude and speed or on the ground. Neither cruising nor waiting on the ground takes much energy or causes the plane much stress.

What does cause the plane a lot of stress is transitions: takeoff and landing.

- At takeoff, engines operate at very high thrust. Sometimes, the airplane vibrates as a result of the very high forces and additional physical phenomena.

- At landing, the plane's gear and body absorb a huge shock when touching down on the runway.

These transition stages are what we call boundary problems, and they need to be carefully dealt with.

Our lives are rich with boundaries. Any parent can tell you about the boundary problems that occur, for example, when his or her first child is born. All of a sudden, the parent is shifted from living a relatively carefree life to being the person responsible for a tiny, loveable, living human being!

Similarly, when the phone rings, that ring signals the interface between the steady state of silence before we answered the phone to the steady state of conversation after we answer it. Transactions of goods vs. payment and teachers passing knowledge to students likewise represent boundaries and interfaces whose quality, efficacy, speed, and so on depend on the parties involved.

Boundaries exist everywhere: between people, mechanical parts, electronic parts and signals, medicine and body, and in many other areas. It is up to us to identify these boundaries and ensure these are properly handled.

Business Convergence

Analyzing convergence of trends helps executives and managers assess the long-term impact of strategic processes like decisions having long-term impact, parts going through extreme temperature cycles, and income convergence over time.

Let's say a company decides to invest in a new sales campaign. The company assumes campaign success and the subsequent increase in sales and profitability. While sales (income) numbers are assumed, projected expenses are quite accurate, leaving a crucial unknown factor: will we achieve the targeted profit? This depends on the campaign results like, will *real* sales grow? Will the product sell at all? Are our sales efforts well targeted?

Because of these and many other unknowns, we will work diligently to *converge* to the planned revenue and profit. Management invests, taking a risk that the return will not be as planned and hoping to recuperate it later.

In 2000, a certain company developed a highly sophisticated xDSL platform for fast internet and telephony infrastructure. The technology was great, but the company's business plan developers failed to address price *trends*. Once the product went into mass use and more competitors entered the market, price naturally dropped—and dropped below 50% of the original price in five years! A convergence analysis of market demand/supply and pricing would have led to the adoption of a different, price flexible[4] strategy or to project closure.

Assessing trends or convergence is important, especially in capital-intensive industries, where oversupply leads many into bankruptcy. Capital-intensive industries—like shipping, airlines, semiconductor R&D, and machine-intensive industries—tend to have trouble meeting business plans. Periodical trend analysis of the respective critical factors should therefore be used as the basis for conceiving and updating business plans.

---

4   Flexibility can be achieved through a modular approach, use of lower cost/performance microprocessors, and so on.

The Boundary Problem as a Management Tool

Convergence is about long-term or strategic trends; the boundary problem is a tactical, short-term tool.

Boundary problems are huge energy consumers and include things like introducing new products, hiring new personnel, phasing out old products, and so on. Daily interface problems are also boundaries including fitting our laptop electrical plugs to electrical outlets in foreign countries, software incompatibility with computers, and cultural and language differences. Cell-phone network compatibility to different transmission systems, and the interface between a wheel and the road are also interfaces. These boundaries require special attention, understanding, and some type of interfacing facility. That is why telecommunications has standards, why friction coefficients of rubber wheels vs. asphalt roads are calculated, and so on.

Between these two tools, convergence and boundaries, decision makers can evaluate opportunities and risks associated with decision making. Risks are measured in terms of personnel, knowhow, time, and money. Once strategic decisions are made, management should define or generate decision filters representing the hard execution rules of said strategy. Additions or changes to such a decision must comply with the filter rules. If they do so smoothly—do it; if not, leave it or revise higher-level decisions.

Corporate Interfaces

Boundaries also exist within companies. There are boundaries related to information sharing, data, goods and funds, and between the four company limbs: Research

& Development, Sales & Marketing, Operations, and Finances.

Interfaces between the different parts of a company are vital, and all sorts of problems erupt when interface management is missing or incomplete. Some symptoms of inept interfaces include over-budgeted R&D programs, underpriced goods, overlooking actual manufacturing costs, under-loading financing and overhead costs and rents, lack of coordination in advertising campaigns, and poor focus of sales messages.

During the 1980s, Digital Equipment Corporation (DEC), which used to pride itself as the second biggest computer company (after IBM), had a display center in its headquarters in Maynard, Massachusetts. In this center DEC demonstrated how their PDP and VAX computers interfaced with IBM ones, transferring data and other information. This was something IBMs couldn't do between their own computer families. Each computer family was developed by a separate R&D team that also developed its own interfaces. A qualitative, later corrected flaw.

Corporate interfaces are where the baton is passed from one runner to the next; they are the seams that hold the garment together. If stitches are falling out, they should be replaced before the hole gets any bigger. As the saying goes, *a stitch in time saves nine.*

Numbers, procedures, and drawings will never compensate for poor staff performance in planning or execution. Good understanding of interfaces, their roles, and how and who should operate them will help companies and organizations thrive.

Analyzing a Company: Time, Funds, and Milestones

The use of intellectual exercises such as analyzing boundaries and extremes is important and highlights issues that require sanity checks. The broader one's thinking and analysis is, the more crucial details will be identified and the sounder the plan will be.

There are three main factors to consider when analyzing a company: time, funds, and milestones.

Time: When planning something, make sure to make extra time allocations to account for contingencies and time-related events like competition, geopolitical events, product markets, monetary issues, and other future effects and threats, internal and external. Where in the timeline should the spare time be allocated is a different question, one that is answered by many existing management theories.

Funding: All projects, companies, and families need funding. Either sufficient funding is available to meet goals or goals must be adjusted to match funding. Fooling oneself by under-budgeting, overspending, and addiction to loans is not a solution; it will only create more problems like Chile, Argentina, Greece, and other countries' financial collapse.

Milestones: Goals are much easier to reach when broken up into reasonable, achievable milestones. Reaching milestones boosts morale, which itself helps push to achieve the next one.

Many startups fail because of enthusiastic over-optimism about time frames, funds, and milestone requirements. Over-optimism, combined with lack of paranoia, is commonplace, and leads entrepreneurs and managers to skip critical details or steps.

This type of intellectual exercise is highly recommended and should not be taken lightly, as complexities and doubts will arise during the process. This process can expose our unconscious creation of *me too*, of shortsightedness or human weaknesses. Those who focus on long-term trends identify details that can kill concepts and will find this an amazing and eye-opening experience.

This qualitative analysis should be repeated periodically during execution to ensure that quantitative execution is in line with the qualitative goals.

Chapter 5:
Qualitative Leadership

The CEO

Chief Executive Officer. Managing Director. General Manager. Whatever title you use for a company's top position is a lonely one, especially in hard times.

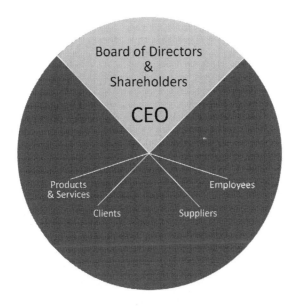

Figure 3 - The CEO, Loneliest of Stars

In most companies, the CEO is the heart and soul, the key person leading the company to success or failure. The CEO's biggest challenges are managing and optimizing short-term corporate efficacy and delivering expected growth and business results while forming and implementing the long-term vision.

CEOs are in charge of the multifaceted interface between shareholders (and the board) and the execution body of the company. CEOs report to a board of directors who approve work plans, control business results, and commend or reprimand the CEO. Once goals, plans, and budgets are agreed upon, CEOs drive their teams to execute and achieve goals—a tricky task by itself. CEOs are the catalysts either initiating execution and change or leading to stagnation and failure.

CEOs and their executives operate in a quicksand environment that forces them to cope with fast-changing technologies, markets, globalization, competition, labor cost, raw material cost, and oil prices. A CEO's wrong decisions or indecision may cost his or her company its existence.

As the lead executive, the CEO of each company is responsible for hiring brains and hands to work, plan, develop, and brand, and for driving the body in a sensible and synchronized motion. In the environment he or she creates, the CEO's personal attitude, ethics, and behavior dictate the type of company he or she leads. Malice draws malice, gossip encourages gossip, fantasy ends in failure, and excessive dominance inspires fear while openness inspires creativity. Goodness is repaid with goodwill, and support is translated into motivation. It is here—in the CEO—that the seeds of failure or success are sown, in his qualitative decisions, part of which is choice of culture and behavior.

CEOs define the futures of their companies by the types of people with whom they surround themselves. Strong personalities hire strong people, people who make up for the CEO's deficiencies so that together, the whole team can push the company ahead. Freedom and a degree of chaos are healthy for creativity—a concept practiced at Google, where employees operate in a quasi-playground environment with few restrictions (as long as they deliver).

Driven by fear or ego, weaker personalities look for lesser subordinates. Weak CEOs define their worth by the comparative incompetence of their teams. Remove such a manager from his fortress, and he shrinks back to his real dimensions.

The attitudes of weaker personalities result in poor teamwork and stagnation, and lead good employees to jump ship in favor of workplaces where they can express themselves and develop. The attitudes of weak managers lead to low motivation and lack of productivity and creativity. Their attitudes also lead to make-believe behaviors like time-consuming gossip, fearful employees idly waiting for instructions, long and useless meetings, paper shuffling, and private internet browsing and game playing. The short-term attitude that engenders such behavior should not be tolerated in leadership positions.

Unlike managers and employees, who can consult their peers and superiors, CEOs do not have many peers to consult with on complex or delicate matters. From his or her lonely position, a CEO has to generate and drive a vision; sell it to employees and shareholders; prove its long-term success; hire and fire; and, overall, deliver results. Surrounded by loneliness, a CEO makes hard decisions.

While many will seek credit for his or her successes, the CEO will have to bear failures alone.

Equipped with a vision and a team, a CEO has to make things happen. If the company is new, the CEO may be surrounded by the positive energy of belief and optimism; if the company is older and large, that energy is normally contained. It is up to the CEO to make sure that spirit, surroundings, ambience, and teamwork are optimized, because those are defining factors in the generation of cooperation, open discussions, communication, and trust. All of these and more are essential for preventing stagnation.

Leaders expect the unexpected and plan for it, because while good news is easy to accept and act upon, the unexpected generates contingencies and confusion. Building, improving, and developing new ideas and ventures are hard, tedious, and time-consuming tasks, while destruction is quick and easy.

Company distress further amplifies the need for leadership, making it lonelier and more challenging. Under distressing circumstances, shareholders lose interest in the company and board members resign to avoid liability in case the company fails. Board members prefer the buck to stop at the CEO's doorstep and for him to deal with financial liabilities, failed products, poor management, and so on. It is up to the CEO of the distressed company to deal with disillusioned, disgruntled, unmotivated employees who worry about losing jobs or not getting salaries due. Changing the course of a ship in troubled waters is possible but challenging, and can be avoided if a company has proper leadership to begin with.

Afraid of the unknown, employees, management, and staff tend to resist changes without offering viable alternatives. The CEO's mental powers, persuasiveness, determination, belief, and leadership are the keys to triggering change and are the power to generate it. It is no coincidence that when a successful CEO leaves a company, share price falls; and when a good CEO joins a troubled company, share price jumps.

In large companies, shareholders, employees, banks, and suppliers have more to lose and therefore tend to be more cooperative with bankruptcy leadership. In smaller companies, this process and the respective support are not as obvious.

Today's mass awareness of the value of good management and decision making makes many followers of the "practices of the successful"—the successful being people like Warren Buffett, Steve Jobs, Bill Gates, Richard Branson, and Jack Welsh. We are keen to imitate their ideas and mechanize them for simplicity, and we often overlook our ability to create our own way to success while hailing the next groundbreaker who dared think out of the box, provide higher levels of integration, and so on.

Theories should be applied only when they fit, and we should learn from the thinking of others. Using only existing theories narrows our imagination and creativity, increasing our dependence on theories of others. We stop solving problems ourselves and instead continuously refer to handbooks. Again—the comparative approach. In a world where everything is personalized (logos, web pages, products, medicine, and so on), we should personalize management to each specific organization. We can generate our own ideas and integrate them with others'. This what our gurus do.

Examples of CEO Leadership Experiences

One Failure

In the year 2000, shortly before the burst of the dot-com bubble, the CEO of a 450-million-dollar sales company wanted to turn the company into a holding company. He spun off technology groups as separate companies with the ultimate goal of developing a new product, selling it, and taking the companies public. Driven by ambition, he promoted the idea to his board of directors and got it approved in spite of two crucial misperceptions. Combined with the dot-com collapse, these misperceptions almost caused the company's demise.

The first misperception was a gross underestimation of the effort, management focus, spin-off costs, and risk of converting safe-haven-seeking employees into entrepreneurs.

The second touched on customer loyalty. While corporate management focused on the newly created start-up companies, corporate clients were taken for granted. This lack of management attention allowed them to be snatched up by competitors.

As corporate costs increased and management attention was spread thin, income and profitability were eroded. The parent company was weakened, barely surviving the dot-com collapse and shrinking to approximately 70 million dollars in sales.

Three Successes

Under Gerald Grinstein's powerful, positive, and decisive leadership, Delta Airlines emerged in 2007 from a two-year bankruptcy. Gerald Grinstein gave a great personal example of how things can be done for the benefit of all. His tenacity and personal sensitivity, combined with strong management and people skills and an understanding of companies and their processes, helped him gain employees' trust. He promised and delivered. He did not daydream or mislead employees. He promised to rehire laid-off Delta employees when times improved, and he did. Why has the previous management failed where Grinstein succeeded? Because of qualitative decisions (or indecision) and lack of people soft skills.

Lee Iacocca engineered the Ford Mustang and the unsuccessful Ford Pinto. His biggest achievement was his revival of the Chrysler Corporation in the 1980s. His success was first and foremost in social terms: he retained jobs and strengthened the "Buy American" motto. He also repaid debts, and shareholders recovered part of their otherwise written-off investment. Here, again, Iacocca received the same organization and company his predecessor had. Why then has he succeeded where others failed?

Percy Barnevik, CEO of the Swedish ASEA conglomerate, successfully merged ASEA with the Swiss-German Brown Boveri Corporation (BBC) forming the ABB Corporation. Both automation and electricity giants were and are strong competitors of US-based General Electric. The merger, with all its risks and complexities, was very successful and benefitted long-term corporate growth.

Expectations and Disappointments

Expectations and disappointments converge at the CEO. It is in the CEO that expectations are generated and responsibility for success or failure lies. A deputy chief of staff of a certain army stated that the 36 steps from his office to the chief of staff's office represent a world of responsibility.

One of the CEO's main tasks is to balance expectations and reality with leadership that combines three characteristics:

- Creating realistic expectations and growth plans with controllable risk levels.

- Helping staff leave their comfort zones and deliver higher-quality results. This involves stifling wishful thinking in favor of useful thinking.

- Making sure financing is in place in the form of ongoing sales, credits, and/or investments.

The damage caused by the absence of these characteristics ripples through shareholders, boards of directors, employees, clients, and other stakeholders. Such disappointments lead to loss of stakeholder backing, loss of sales, lower trust, and dropping share price, reflecting badly on the company's leadership and future.

The Unholy Trinity

The CEO is chosen and appointed by the board of directors, which represents the company's shareholders.

Well-run companies have strong boards with capable and experienced people able and willing to hire a strong and influential CEO—and remove a failing or weak CEO. Unfortunately, not all companies are well-run, and not all boards are strong. Weak boards often elect weak, underperforming CEOs, eventually losing shareholder trust.

Why would any board elect a weak CEO? For any number of reasons. For example, a controlling shareholder might want to exploit the company and therefore appoint someone he thinks will follow his orders—including those against company interests. Will the rest of the board members stand up to him? Will the CEO practice his duty to serve the company's best interests? Will shareholders intervene and force change and improvement? Who will stand up and absorb the fire for the rest of the participants? Such conflicts are typical in family-owned companies, especially when the second generation takes over. They also occur in startups with dominant entrepreneurs lacking managerial skills, government-owned enterprises, and others.

Sometimes, the reverse can happen. Instead of a dominant shareholder and a weak CEO, there is a dominant CEO and a weak board. In this case, the CEO can play on the fears of the board to maintain power even when he's doing a bad job. He may, for instance, threaten that if he leaves the company, the company will collapse. A weak board will try to negotiate with the CEO and then end up following his vagaries and whims, perpetuating the CEO's power and the board's weakness.

In any case, if a company is doing poorly, the board of directors should not rely on the CEO's assessment; it should independently analyze the source of a negative turn, form its own opinion, and, if the CEO is the problem, relieve him of his position. This is one of the reasons that good board members are always exposed to the VP level, talking and listening to them as well.

ENRON is an example of a strong and manipulative management that lost its way. Certain top management personalities changed corporate priorities from the wellbeing of the company to the presentation of good results to Wall Street investors, thereby increasing their public esteem. ENRON's management succeeded in branding itself as a successful, growth-oriented, shareholder value-building management. However, its self-branding was a lie, and ENRON created one of the biggest accounting frauds ever. The management of the company that *Fortune* magazine named America's Most Innovative Company cost its 22,000 employees their jobs and the accounting firm Arthur Andersen its existence. Huge collateral damage affected thousands of people, from cleaners and food suppliers to agents, sales representatives, and energy suppliers. Many of these people found new jobs or continued with the divisions of ENRON that were acquired by third parties, but many others were left jobless.

A company is like a child to the owners or shareholders, to be nurtured, taught, fed, developed, and strengthened. The goal is to bring this child up with good health, positive values, and tools so it can lead a long, independent life. For healthy growth, non-productive elements like power plays and breaches of trust should be avoided.

To keep the trinity of shareholders, board members, and CEO healthy and to ensure company success, the *only* consideration in decision making should be the long-term wellbeing of the company. The company's success is also the success of its shareholders, employees, suppliers, and clients.

Leadership vs. Administration

In many instances, the role of management is misperceived, being looked upon and applied as the art of administration rather than the art of vision and leadership. Short- or even medium-term survival of administrative management is possible in healthy, well-operating companies, thriving markets, or monopolistic businesses. Real leadership is needed in growth companies and must be the forefront during downturns and tough cycles. Not all administrative managers will survive crises; however, some poor administrators may emerge as tough and decisive leaders.

Most leaders have broad global horizons and are able to generate visions and unite their teams to achieve their goals. Leaders build to last. They avoid building companies whose only purpose is to be sold, because doing that would shift their attention from nurturing and growing the company to looking for buyers. Leaders focus, form a vision, hire people, bring tools, and then turn execution over to the administrators.

Cisco is an example of such careful, overall planning and execution. Whereas Lucent and Nortel practically disappeared as a result of the 2001 burst of the bubble, Cisco not only survived but emerged stronger.

CEOs need not necessarily be creative; they can seek creativity in others who are better able to conceive new and original ways to become winners. They search for people who avoid stagnation and avoid *planning for the last war* by using old, outdated methodologies. When the leader's role is undertaken by an administrator's personality, chances are that the company will start running into what I refer to as an *efficient stagnation* where all activities are executed, check-lists followed but with no results.

The Mountain Parable

As humans, we tend to prefer paved roads, comfort zones, and consensus. If the road is in the midst of the valley, we will follow it comfortably, not necessarily knowing what awaits us. Every now and then, it is advisable to climb up a hill or mountain along the road and scan the horizon and the paths leading to your target. Once the target is identified, you can decide on the best way to reach it. It is important to verify that your targets are still realistic, taking into account things like environments, competition, technologies, markets, and other ever-changing parameters.

Scanning the horizon requires an intellectual effort, especially when seeking unbiased thinking. Decision makers have to overcome the tendency to justify what has been done rather than courageously look ahead at what is the right thing to do. Moreover, it is not always the highest intellectual hill or mountain we climb to scan the horizon. Repeating this hill-climbing mental exercise from time to time helps sharpen and focus targets and goals and—equally as important—how to reach them.

Paved roads are where comfort levels are higher than gravel roads or no roads. This is because someone else performed preliminary work that you can use as a reference or baseline.

The dot-com bubble is one example of well-tested technology combined with impatient sellers. Market surveys based on interviews with optimistic managements were conducted; and, as time went by, hype grew and risks were perceived as lower and lower when in fact they were increasing. In retrospective, the real winners were the early birds, those who created the real change and did not follow already ploughed patterns. Early birds had no market surveys available as there was no market; they had no readymade components or waiting and eager clients.

The early birds were the real pioneers whose investment multipliers were higher. Yes, some failed, but it was the followers who increased competition, leading to sharp price reductions and to eventual oversupply.

Business Plans

A business plan is a formal document listing the business's goals, plans, and means for reaching those goals, along with background information. Business plans also detail how much time and money are required to reach each corporate milestone. In other words, they are basically a combination of each of our four steps—high-level goal/vision, grand strategy, execution strategy, and tactical execution.

While business plans are commonplace tools for attracting investors, they should first and foremost be written for the company's internal needs. The business plan is the anchor and pivot around which the company evolves until otherwise decided. Business plans must be realistic and clarify the assumptions on which they are based. As time goes by, assumptions should be rechecked, verified, or adjusted (more sanity checks), making the business plan a living and breathing document.

Business plans are about selling products and making profits. By increasing financing within the limits of the law of diminishing returns, some activities can be accelerated, shortening execution times. The advantage in shortening execution times is that doing so reduces overhead costs and time to market, which means that products are more modern when introduced to the market. Attempts to reduce costs by reducing investments and prolonging development and product introduction times are therefore not recommended.

Business plans do not need to be long. They need to be concise and easy to read, understand, and implement. In an attempt to convince the reader (or the writer) of the validity of business plan assumptions, writers tend to elaborate more than necessary. Typical wording includes such phrases as "we believe that," "the trend is," "we estimate," and "market forecasts." Here again, care has to be taken to make sure assumptions are realistic and have a high probability of surviving time, competition, emerging alternatives, and market changes in terms of cost reduction, competition, branding, differentiators, and other key factors.

Contrary examples where full-fledged business plans are put aside also exist. One successful example is that of the owner of a plastic products company with 700 million dollars in annual sales. To avoid confusion created by business plans, the owner does not share the full company budget; he only shares the sales budget. His argument is that if he shared the full company budget, management and employees would make sure they spent every penny budgeted for expenses while not necessarily meeting the sales budget.

The Split Personality

Executives and managers need to develop a split personality to ensure long-term growth and success.

The first personality is short term. On a daily basis, executives and managers have to be cautious and run and operate companies as if financial resources were scarce. "Sales need to be increased, overspending avoided, staff size controlled, risky inventory-buildup prevented. Every dollar spent has to be directly related to an income to be generated." While the logic behind this personality is simple, one must take care not to convey pessimism. Your message should be agility, efficiency, and effectiveness that make the best use of your resources. It is a corporate culture.

The second personality is long term. It is that of the optimist driving the vision. "The company has a bright future; we will invest today to reap our rewards tomorrow!" Investments require spending to generate the future and hopefully will not become misspent funds. Development of new products, new markets, reduced manufacturing costs, and other such factors should have a pre-assessed potential return on investment. Purchasing overpriced parts, services, or over-fancy offices has no real return on investment, at least not in industry.

Split personality is, in short, about short term versus long term, caution versus optimism, and spending versus investing.

Transparency and Accessibility

Transparency, though perceived by many as a weakness, is a powerful management tool. Transparency is a lubricant for company wheels. It drastically reduces internal frictions and second guessing, reduces uncertainty and increases trust, reduces and even avoids gossip (which is time-consuming and therefore expensive), leads to money and time savings, and increases motivation—resulting in higher productivity and efficiency.

Transparency is not about becoming a vigilante, micromanaging employees, or attempting to pull or push employees to meet company goals; it is a motivator and trust builder that gives employees a back wind and peace of mind. It further increases output because when employees realize that they can reach goals, they become driven by the power of their own successes.

Transparency is also about keeping employees informed of the corporate sales and finances that they helped generate. This is especially true during downturns and periods of uncertainty. Transparency reduces perceived uncertainty and is interpreted as honesty. Honest people can be trusted. Employees work hard knowing that they can trust management to protect them and share the truth with them.

Transparency is nurtured by creating a dialogue with employees and by being accessible. Executives and managers are surprised how much one can learn about one's company from the people *down there*. Employees have a lot of information that can be exploited— information that can be used to discover new product features, improve manufacturing processes, and come up with new product ideas. Accessibility does not break managerial or organizational structures; it is about listening and cooperating, about people and information exchange.

A disastrous example of lack of accessibility and transparency cost Israel dearly during the October 1973 war. Field intelligence reported that the Egyptians were accumulating forces along the Suez Canal. Intelligence indicated that these forces were more than just military maneuver forces. An Egyptian spy, Ashraf Marwan, President Nasser's son-in-law, warned the Israeli Mossad 40 hours before the war of its beginning. This and more information reached the chief of army intelligence, who, instead of sharing it with his superiors, disregarded it. He had indoctrinated himself to the point of rejecting whatever information did not fit his doctrine. Having no additional decision makers able to review the raw information, Israel was caught off guard. This gross and costly error was a result of ego, lack of communications, and inaccessibility of the lower ranks to decision makers before the war begun. As a result of this fiasco, major changes were made to ensure it could not happen again.

Education and Leadership

Managers form the human infrastructure on which a company is built. Management is the heart and skeleton around which employees, technologies, products, drive and muscle, brains and thinking are grown. This is why good managements create good companies.

There is a tendency to seek managers with advanced academic degrees and titles. Some such managers are great experts in their fields but poor visionaries or executives, so elements other than academics should also be taken into consideration.

Managers need to plan and lead execution, and in certain cases they need to be visionaries and intrapreneurs.[5] Managers should have people skills, strong leadership, execution, sales, troubleshooting, and hire-and-fire abilities. They should understand business environments, markets, and cultures. These elements don't necessarily depend on education; some great business leaders throughout history barely made it through high school, and others were great academics whose success was a result of leadership, vision, and drive complemented by expert knowhow.

On the one hand, education—and especially wide knowledge—can be very helpful. Analysis and integration of general information helps develop a *feeling* as to the direction in which a company should be steered within the environment. General knowledge provides hints to global opportunities and threats.

---

5   An initiator *within* an organization.

On the other hand, academic studies represent certain risks. In the course of academic studies, students study and learn those subjects taught at a given point in time—and learn information that may be biased or proven to be wrong as science develops. Furthermore, in most areas of expertise, information will become outdated within 10 or 15 years. When not kept up, education may become a short-term enabler but a long-term millstone.

What's far more helpful is learning *how* to think—which goes back to our discussion on thinking out of the box. By expanding your horizons through general subjects and developing people skills, visions, daring, judgments, and execution abilities, employees and managers alike can continuously improve themselves as people and as professionals.

Ultimately, the best person to hire for a leadership role is the one able to exploit his or her persona and create an ever-expanding educational process.

Chapter 6:
Qualitative Decisions Gone Wrong

Throughout this book, qualitative decisions are shown to be an important contributor to success. The *quantitative* aspects of running a business are a reflection of *qualitative* decisions like late layoffs or the stopping or revamping of unprofitable product lines. These decisions, or indecisions, are people driven and in many cases reflect decision-maker wishes rather than realistic approaches. This chapter shares some life experiences in which qualitative decisions, or their timing, led to failure.

Where Is the Market?

Let us look again at the xDSL equipment company discussed in Chapter 4. It had a sister company involved in internet security infrastructure. The former operated in a saturated market while the latter lacked market understanding. We decided to merge them.

While preparing the merger, I identified two major flaws in the internet equipment business model, or rather the qualitative decisions behind the model. First, the target market, telephone companies, represented a total of maybe 1,000 potential clients for a few systems each.

Therefore, the market was too small to justify the R&D investment. Second, the next-generation product on which the company's future relied was based on old technologies that clients would refrain from buying. The chief technical officer (CTO) justified choice of older technologies by stating that the first product developed is only a proof of concept, not the product itself. While the product concept was viable, the CTO's execution strategy was unjustified because of the double investment in proof of concept and product (60 engineers over two years).

Once the merge was completed, the product model was changed, targeting the massive corporate market and adopting the most advanced technological platform. The result was a smaller, lower-cost platform; more clients; less regulation; and a drastic shortening of time to market. The uniqueness of the new offering led to sales based on the prototype units. A year later, this company was merged into a telecom equipment conglomerate.

Before the merger, the two companies were failing due to poor qualitative decisions. In order for the newly merged company to thrive, I needed to change the qualitative reasoning behind it by optimally combining the strengths of each.

The Spin of Extracting Value

In the year 2000, the board of directors of a 500-million-dollar company decided to extract value from the corporation by spinning off its larger divisions as independent companies, each of which would be taken public once the process was completed. The qualitative risks of this step were improperly assessed if at all.

The board and executives were so keen on "making more money" that they chose to underestimate the time, funds, and especially the management attention such a step would consume. Management attention included issues like financial structure, legal, technology ownership, equipment ownership, employee wishes to join a company or not, and so on. The divisions-to-become-companies were slowed down, further increasing costs.

Secondly, as a corporation, the company provided a unified offering with complementary product lines. When it became separate companies, clients would need to split their purchases and discussions among three companies. This important edge led many clients to one-stop-shop competitors.

Furthermore, a) the board of directors decided to take the companies public (IPO) in the year 2000, on the verge of the dot-com bubble; however, management failed to identify their saturated markets; and b) the board did not learn from the experience of similar companies that retained their economies of scale and financial strength.

The burst of the bubble caught the company off guard and spun it into a vicious circle of no money, poor finances, and no expansion in collapsing markets. On the other hand, having lost their pensions, small investors opted to increase their savings, and institutional investors stopped investing until the skies cleared. The board retraced its steps, reconsolidating the group; firing managers; and absorbing, for the second time, huge reorganization losses in a shrinking market.

Who Is the Salesperson?

The CEO of a telecom equipment company was in love with reorganizations. In one of them, he insisted on having sales leadership broken down into five positions of vice president of sales, each reporting to the respective division managers, who themselves were former R&D people with no real sales experience.

The concept yielded poor results due to poor qualitative reasoning: a) four of the divisions shared the same potential clients, and it made no sense to have four different salespeople call on each client; b) the very competitive marketplace required market leadership not technology leadership; and c) the split crippled sales leaders' ability to have a unified and coherent view of the market, its challenges, and its opportunities.

The CEO refused to have a single central sales and marketing function, thus diverging sales efforts. When the bubble burst, the company was caught unprepared and shrank dramatically in sales, unable to leverage synergies to increase sales.

Asking the Wrong Question

The HR vice president of a traditional-industry billion-dollar corporation decided to enrich the knowledge and tools of the company's executives and managers. With its being a traditional company, managers had each worked for the company for a minimum of 10 years and up to 35 years.

The VP hired an organizational consultant to interview the potential participants to find out "what additional knowledge and skills they wished to develop."

The logic behind hiring the organizational consultant was flawed to begin with because the employees had been living in the same environment for so long that they had no basis for comparison. They didn't really know anything else, so how could they ask for it? The correct approach would have been to map existing knowledge and identify what additional knowledge was a) missing and b) could positively impact the company results.

Follow your own Rules

The management of an oil-and-gas underwater-pipe-laying corporation found that most of its projects were in trouble. Projects were between 50 to 250 million dollars each, and the problems cut deeply into profitability.

The company's operational structure was in what is called a matrix structure with central departments doing work for, and providing services to project teams. Seeing the problems in project execution, top management brought in a series of project management consultants, who did not solve the problems.

After 18 months of work I joined the team, studying the information and work done so far, and I chose to increase the radius of thinking. I expanded beyond project execution, also studying pre-project activities. It turned out that the seeds of the problem had been sown in the earlier bid stage and the way the transition from bid win to project initiation was handled.

With simple, counter-dramatic focusing steps and two new hires, the problem was solved for new projects. Once the strategic problem was solved, we focused again on the tactical execution of the older and troubled projects.

Chapter 7:
Working with People

Working with people and getting them to positively contribute to success requires a human touch that I would summarize as:

- Be humble.

- Don't condescend.

- All people react positively to warmth, openness, listening, and understanding.

Those three tools massively improve communications and teamwork. So why don't more people use them? Because daily pressures make it easy to lose sight of such principles of human relationship.

Managements need to drive people to operate in a quicksand environment where the only constant is change, in some fields more than others. People make the change and sustain the company with technologies, markets, globalization, competition, and lower labor and raw-material costs. And, although they are more demanding, people awareness and sensitivity are two of the best tools managements have to create better teams and more flexibility. People awareness helps convince others to leave comfort zones, change the inertia, and adopt different habits and mechanics.

Delegation

Delegation begins with trust—which is the cornerstone of delegating responsibility and authority. Yet sometimes delegation suffers from poor implementation like delegation of responsibility without authority, which creates orphan failures and multi-parent successes. Wrongful implementation mostly reflects on the personalities involved—their egos, fears, wills, and dreams.

If there is trust between you and your employees, then yield, give way, and hand over authority as well. People want to feel trusted, to prove themselves, to initiate, and to make things happen. They possess the *can do, will do* attitude, which they will apply if mutual trust exists.

Delegating executives are far more successful than those who reprimand, micromanage, or mismanage their employees. They develop faster-moving, better-motivated, and profitable organizations. As a result, executives and employees have more energy and are more efficient, better prepared, and more motivated to take calculated risks. They are willing to spend their energies in markets and on the offering rather than in creating internal friction and controls.

The benefits, however, aren't without an element of risk. The more a manager delegates, the harder and more complex supervision and control tasks become. The cost of errors might be higher but it is compensated by a faster moving organization and less errors. Moreover, since delegation is to trusted, can- do- will- do employees, positive results can be expected especially as their experience grows.

Communication is key here, as are cross-checking information and verifying reported results by comparing them with supporting numbers and plans, features, sales, and other important information. Let your employees also have open discussions with their peers and increase the circle of trust.

London's Barings Bank is a sobering example of what happens when delegation is performed without communication and when proper controls—managerial, auditing, and reading between the lines—aren't in place.

In 1995, Barings Bank went bankrupt as a result of a manager's trust in the employee Nick Leeson, who was in charge of arbitrage trading at the Singapore branch. As Nick Leeson expressed it, "People at the London end of Barings were all so 'know-it-all' that nobody dared ask a stupid question in case they looked silly in front of everyone else."

What doomed the bank wasn't delegation in principle; it was the cultural flaw in the organization (as explained by Leeson) that caused controls and limited human-to-human communications.

Controls and supervision must be complemented by communication between people: employees, clients, suppliers, and other stakeholders. Foxhole attitudes in which people barricade themselves with their information and knowhow are crippling. Teamwork requires cooperation and sharing of information to grease the wheels and improve the organization. Uncooperative people should be isolated and their responsibilities should be narrowed down if their value rules out firing them.

Cooperation is also about tolerance. Let ten trivial or "stupid" questions be asked rather than miss one important question. Once questions are asked, answers should be evaluated at the source of the question or problem. (Again, looking at the root of a problem, not just at its symptoms.) Being tolerant drastically improves the probability of identifying a mistake in the course of developing a solution, project, product, or design.

Trust-building contributes an additional advantage: the positive energies of happy and self-fulfilled people, and helps sustain efforts to keep up with constant change. Devote the little extra, like the *spice of love* that makes the difference in Granny's soup. Treat others as you would like to be treated.

Unfortunately, as much as we would like to fully trust everybody, not everybody can be trusted in one aspect or another. One type of employee that cannot be trusted is the *why not*. Why-not employees focus on why something cannot be done, an attitude normally accompanied by detailed and tiring explanations. The why-not attitude is a poisonous self-fulfilling prophecy—which means that why-not employees will usually fail when trusted.

Ultimately, it takes two to delegate: the delegating and the receiving parties. If the receiving party is not up to accepting responsibility, then he or she is not your growth partner. Delegation and acceptance are the privileges of sound and trusting personalities.

Motivating People

Motivation is a key success factor. Motivated people are happier people, radiating positive energies and attitudes. Such people are inviting, magnetizing, fun to work with, and easier to follow. Motivated people serve clients better, are more focused, and effectively serve the high good of the company and its stakeholders.

Environment

Motivation is achieved by creating a good environment with good attitudes. Praise is given when justified, support and advice when needed, constructive criticism when warranted, and the right backing when errors are made. Motivation is also affected by general atmosphere, recognition, by involving families and communities, supporting employees through hardships, and visiting them in happiness and sadness.

Benefits

Thomas Watson's IBM increased employee loyalty by institutionalizing employee development, healthcare, contributions to pension funds, schooling, and so on. The results of this employee-care program are still reaped today.

Gratitude

Treat employees well, and they'll work better; their higher motivation increases end-product quality and reduces client complaints and product returns. Lack of motivation causes inefficiencies in, for example, time, costs, quality, and product features. Here again, just like with trust and delegation, it is Granny's intangible *spice of love* without which the same ingredients taste differently.

For communitarian reasons, the owner of an aluminum workshop decided to employ deaf and hearing-impaired people on the production and assembly floors. Their motivation and gratitude are reflected in improved product quality, fewer errors, and higher-than-average productivity. The equation is simple: help and be helped.

Patience

Be patient and don't expect immediate results from a new assignment; let subordinates concentrate on progress and results rather than reporting to and appeasing the boss.

Suitability

Make sure employees are engaged in activities they excel at and can succeed at. When an employee is not suited to a job, making both him and management frustrated, the employee should be moved to a different job. If nothing is available to suit the employee, sometimes the best thing for both employee and company is to ask the employee to leave.

Success is a self-motivator, a catalyst leading to higher, more effective and efficient outputs. Motivated people are willing to undertake more responsibility, make decisions, and defend and execute them. When employees needs a push to believe in themselves, help them succeed and increase their self-esteem and self-confidence—which will lead to a positive motivational cycle.

The Golden Rule

Above all, treat employees as humans, and they'll reciprocate by performing their tasks with higher accuracy and care, improving end-product quality and reducing client complaints and product returns. Employees treated like objects will see their employer only as a source of income, not as a fellow human, and will therefore be less motivated.

Values

When management maintains values, so do employees. Employees are more motivated and fulfilled when they have something in common with management and with other teams.

Values are the fusion-factor of humans in their daily environments. Private and public companies with positive values show better performance and sustainability than companies without values. An example of a company whose leadership lost its values is ENRON.

Positive values like credibility, honesty, trustworthiness, decisiveness, focus, humor, communications, listening, and accepting others are catalysts to success. They keep companies on sustainable growth paths and increase employee loyalty. Choose employees who share your values, and you will be chosen by those employees in return.

Communicating With People

Humans are the most complex animals on Earth. Our highly developed communication skills are the epicenter of our social and professional lives. Different people have different behaviors, languages, cultures, sensitivities, and other defining characteristics. Getting to know and understand another person—his or her sensitivities, language, and culture—is key to communications.

When communicating to achieve a goal, seek to resolve the other party's concern, whether it's based on ego or language or real needs. Be positive and don't let confrontational behaviors rise unnecessarily.

In certain circumstances, confrontations are necessary to affect thoughts, actions, and feelings; but they must be done in an appropriate way. Be smart; don't respond to aggressiveness with the same. Take charge, and be decisive and persistent to achieve your goals in spite of the derailing attitudes of the other party. Be polite but firm, follow your company's behavioral policy, and enforce it justly—not out of anger. Give the person a chance to apologize; everyone loses his or her temper sometimes. And if a person's attitude becomes damaging, fire him or her.

Listening is also a wonderful communication tool. First-line people such as field salespeople, manufacturing floor people, and R&D teams have valuable information; they are a source of innovation and improvement, and they are the execution power.

For example, when listening to your employees, you might find that assembly times can be reduced, secretaries can speed processes, and service technicians can integrate field-collected information into actionable items. Furthermore, when executives listen, employees are proud—even more so when the executive publicly praises them. And their success is yours.

Listening and communicating are the cornerstones of the executive-employee relationship. Companies are not democracies, but they nevertheless have, or should have, forums for employees to share their ideas. Such forums can have professional or social goals. It is not a coincidence that democracies[6] have survived totalitarian monarchies and dictators, and that the world's greatest companies grow and thrive under free-initiative, free-speech forms of democracy.

Working Globally

In practical terms, our business world became smaller as a result of twentieth-century developments in transportation and communications. "I am only an email away" is a reality

---

6 "Democracy is the worst form of government except for all those others that have been tried." – Winston Churchill

that allows us to achieve much more in one day now than we could two decades ago. Stock trading is managed in microseconds rather than fractions of an hour. Shipment of goods is done overnight; funds transfer in minutes. Industries are global, as are their clients.

When working globally, understanding other cultures is of great importance. For example:

Japanese are non-confrontational and therefore will avoid giving negative answers. They will instead offer alternatives. This can be frustrating and irritating on both sides: Americans don't understand that the Japanese, by offering alternatives, are saying *no*; and the Japanese don't understand why the Americans won't take no for an answer.

The Turkish prolong negotiations prior to closing deals.

Latin Americans base business relationships on personal rapport.

There are cultures in which a signed agreement is considered a recommendation for the business framework and the business itself has to be conducted over drinking and dining to ensure its proper execution. There are other cultures in which a signed agreement is absolute.

In different countries, different hand gestures may mean different things—and a gesture that is positive in one country may be negative or offensive in another. In Italy, foreigners are generally advised never to use hand gestures, because Italians have a complex body language based around hand gestures, and ignorant use is confusing when not outright rude.

When interacting with people from other cultures, research and understand the way they perceive the interaction. You have your interpretation; do you understand theirs? Like in any business negotiation, success depends on understanding the other party, his or her thinking, goals, limitations, culture, how badly he or she wants the deal, and so on.

One of Sememe's investors was a major Japanese corporation. I got to work with the corporation when I was CEO, which gave me a first-hand experience of how cultural nuances can affect business.

Sememe dealt primarily with a specific representative from the Japanese company, the mentor promoting both us within the corporation and our products in the market. At a certain point during our relationship, I sensed a change in the speed at which the mentor responded to our emails, and I became worried when email answers stopped altogether. I was worried because not answering emails is rude in Japanese culture, so something must have happened. But what? I waited patiently, and after two months, we received an email from our mentor apologizing for not answering the emails. He informed us that he was leaving the company and introduced his replacement.

This meant Sememe was facing another uphill battle: we had to resell our company to the new mentor so he'd drive sales and keep us high on the Japanese company's to-do list.

We welcomed the new mentor and offered assistance with studying our product line and its benefits. As time went by, our new mentor, instead of updating us on his sales plans, politely delegated to us the job of putting together the business plan for sales in Japan. I also noted that he copied all his subordinates on the emails but skipped his superiors.[7]

---

7 It is customary in many Japanese companies to copy the full hierarchy on certain types of emails.

I needed a response strategy—non-confrontational, polite, and positive. I decided to agree with all his requests; and, to fulfill his requests, I asked for his help with information we needed. I made sure to copy his superiors as well as his subordinates on the emails. This was a test of patience, six months of useless to-and-fro correspondence. Then, one day, the Japanese gentleman called under instructions from his CEO. He asked for our permission to fly over and apologize in person for his behavior.

What had happened was this: the new Japanese manager had different product-selling priorities of which we were not part. Being non-confrontational as Japanese are, he avoided telling us the negative news, expecting us to let their commitments fade away. During his visit, we terminated our representation agreement, receiving a hefty compensation and gaining our freedom to reinitiate sales in the Japanese market.

Corporate Politics

Corporate politics, especially in medium and small organizations, can be destructive. Politics lead to battle language: me vs. you, us vs. them—when one should be concentrating on we and us. Language and behaviors move from top to bottom. If the boss gossips, then gossip becomes a norm; if he is always behind closed doors, then a closed-door, separatist culture develops. An inquisitive boss develops inquisitive teams.

Medium and small companies suffer the most from politics. On a minor level, politics may sometimes lead to healthy internal competition; but beyond a reasonable level, politics increase internal friction, double efforts, and needlessly spend energies. This can be stopped or contained through generous personal example and leadership.

Managers should frequently tour their facilities, offices, manufacturing floors, outlets, warehouses, and other business-related locations. They should communicate with everyone, sending a message of accessibility and receptiveness to important information, anytime and anywhere. This is what HP's founders did in its early days: they were attentive to improvement and growth ideas, accessible, and fostered communications and teamwork. It was massively successful.

Prove to your staff that this system works by having an open flow of information from bottom to top. To avoid undermining authority, instructions should flow down through the organizational hierarchy.

Encourage people to identify and report problems as early as possible. It is easier to contain small problems earlier than bigger problems later. The cost of correcting a problem increases tenfold with every additional progress step. Putting in a new one-cent component can prevent a thousand-dollar replacement in the field. Most mass automotive recalls are the result of some low-cost, unthought-of defect.

Reduce Bureaucracy

By writing, reading, answering, and filing, people overload themselves with paper to the point of inefficiency. Some managers stick to detailed written reporting. Such managers are the administrative, paranoid type seeking to cover their backs. Others avoid discussions and brainstorming, hate being bothered with details (even if critical), and would rather communicate entirely in writing.

Excessive use of writing creates a big burden on the organization, because:

- People spend time writing documents, reports, and emails.

- Other people spend time reading them.

- Writers wait for answers, prolonging the dialogue.

- Everybody is busy filing and managing their filing systems.

- Ineffectively written arguments and discussions take place.

- Written documents are much more likely to be misunderstood.

- Human dynamics are lost—which means that so is the brainstorming effect—the effect in which one person makes a comment that develops into a whole new idea.

On top of these problems, there are direct costs of secretaries, paper, ink, filing cabinets, and space.

Symptoms of organizations with excessive bureaucracy include people stuck at their desks, no hallway discussions, and ineffective internal phone calls. Pretexts like "I will send you a memo" slow down organizations. (However, those same slow-moving employees will be very efficient and punctual when it comes to lunch and coffee breaks.)

Talk, communicate, think out of the box, and think and behave as a leader, not as a servant keen to serve his boss's whims. The Almighty blessed us with two ears and one mouth, so we should listen twice as much as we talk. Listening is learning; it is about understanding others while sharing the common goal of generating growth.

An owner of a large manufacturing (only) company visited a high-tech company. Upon his return, he commented that he couldn't understand how those people made money. "Everybody is standing and talking in the hallways!" He didn't understand that human trust and interaction reduce bureaucracy and accelerate processes.

Sememe had the habit of generating paper. Upon joining, I asked executives and managers to bring a list of their pending tasks to our one-on-one meetings. Following the then-existing corporate culture, the managers came with two copies of their task list and a written report. This excess was part of the executives' and managers' gross misunderstanding of their responsibilities. Their time was wasted on writing useless documents.

Too much paper shifts people from their goals and causes exponentially growing inefficiency—on top of the direct costs and the environmental effect. Not every meeting is a presentation, nor does it require hours of preparation. Either you know your numbers or you don't. Keep communications simple. Deliver what you have to deliver and avoid overselling yourself. If nothing else, overselling may be interpreted as compensation for lack of performance.

In Sememe, I replaced the bad paper habit with emailing concise, prioritized information up to half a page in length. No more irrelevant written reports or lengthy meeting summaries. The list of high-level goals was handwritten, updated manually during the meeting, and brought back to the next meeting with all past comments on it. This technique has proven very effective.

Ultimately, good communication is about trust. If you don't trust your managers, fire them—don't become their secretary, policeman, or micromanager.

Minimize Overlap

Goodwill and lack of defined responsibilities lead people to do others' jobs as well as their own (see also Chapter 8 on Delegation of Incompetence). If a salesperson manages inventory, he or she is not selling. If a product manager does sales, he or she is not looking ahead to improve competitive edges.

Within a company, its divisions, and all phases of the business, efficiency is gained by minimizing activity overlap between different functions.

Minimization still must keep interfaces working properly (see Chapter 4). The managerial challenge is to create supporting infrastructures that enable efficient communication and effective execution flow. Nowadays, most interfaces are computerized and, when correctly designed, allow access to all relevant stakeholders and provide internal controls.

Lack of internal controls leads to misunderstandings. The challenge of minimization is to define working interfaces—whether manual, verbal, or computerized—to achieve effective flow between corporate functions, decision makers, and executing employees. Keep structures simple, minimize internal friction and inefficient use of energies, and focus all corporate energies to serving and supporting clients.

Simplifying management systems is a complex task. Implementing and assimilating the new system may be challenging, because employees will need to change their habits.

Software companies like Oracle and SAP have made a fortune selling business software packages targeting such interfaces. Investing in one of these packages quickly pays off in the form of a more efficient, better-controlled, better-planned, and faster-moving company. It will also leave more time for personal interaction to discuss important issues rather than technicalities.

Firing People

Firing people is a must. It is part of Darwin's law of evolution by natural selection in a company. Firing people improves the staff while maintaining a message of excellence and integrity. If you are consistent and moral about firing only incompetent, dishonest, or slacking employees, then doing so should create no dilemma.

It is harder when you need to sacrifice good, honest, and hardworking people due to cost cuts, but firing these people is still necessary—the alternative is going bankrupt and sacrificing all your employees. This doesn't make firing good people easy, but it justifies it.

Here are some issues to consider when firing people:

Be sensitive but determined.

Explain clearly and graciously the reasons for termination and end the relationship on the best possible terms. That former employee will be out there, communicating with remaining employees, friends, and family and serving as a former company ambassador. Fair departures are appreciated and help avoid demoralization and defamation.

After dismissals take place, explain to the team why the individual has been dismissed. The importance of such explanations, which should not be personal or detailed, is in the attention to employees, in the sharing with them, and in the message that management reports to employees as much as employees report to management.

Chapter 8:
Delegation of Incompetence

The delegation of authority and responsibility is a known practice. However, it is not the only type of delegation. There is delegation of incompetence as well: a dangerous approach touched by ego, fear, or naivety. Behind it lie reasons such as not admitting inability, fear of failure, laziness, or corporate politics.

Many managers and employees tend to get rid of hot potatoes by delegating them under sophisticated pretexts and expecting others to either a) do the work for them or b) steer the delegator to the decision to be made.

In this context, *incompetence* refers to the gap between responsibilities and abilities, required and actual knowhow, and experience. This chapter describes typical cases in which people are wrongfully delegating their responsibilities, whether they realize it or not.

Consultants

Managers are making poor or unjustified use of their consultants when they expect them to do things they weren't hired for—such as providing leadership or deciding things for them. To properly use consultants, managers need to identify specific needs and assign the consultants to bridge specific knowledge, ability, or time gaps.

Take, for example, a well-known US corporation whose management decided to reduce corporate costs. Targeting 20% savings, the corporation hired one of the top consulting firms to analyze where cost reductions could be made. The consulting firm sent in a group of young analysts to study the organization and collect data and information. Upon seeing the initial data and rightfully assuming that client executives would oppose such cuts, the lead consultants recommended an increased cost reduction target, assuming it would be internally negotiated down to the required 20%. Months went by before the study and planning were concluded, and thus decision making went into limbo awaiting the report. When management received the report, they had to read it and implement the recommendations according to their understanding of the report. The result was chaos and no real savings. The poor result was affected by loss of corporate momentum, employee slowdowns, focus deflection, and implementation of the recommendations with a different understanding from what the consultants meant.

How could this happen? The problem was that the company's top management delegated its incompetence—that is, its ignorance about its own company—to the consulting firm and then accepted the firm's recommendations without even analyzing the results. Top management, knowing which activities are vital and which not, knowing priorities and other considerations, should have led the cost-cutting analysis and implementation, not delegated the task out. This should have and could have been done without deflecting the company's focus from its real goals and commitments. Management opted for someone to tell it what to do, to lead it.

Failure in such cases is inevitable for several reasons:

- Consultants are not bound or expected to know the company better than its role-fulfilling management.

- Consultants write reports and propose actions based on *their* understanding of the company and on their filters, education, experience, and understanding.

- Management and staff implement consultants' recommendations through their reader filters and experience.

- The process is time consuming when consultants collect information, write reports, and negotiate their recommendations with management. Management in turn can identify major flaws and deal with them while studying and planning the next step.

The gaps between understanding and interpretation lead to divergence from the consultants' originally intended results.

Furthermore, use of consultants as part of managements' unaware delegation of incompetence triples incurred costs. These include:

- Direct consultant costs, including employee time and defocus during interviews.

- The time it takes management and employees to read and implement the conclusions, which slows down the company.

- Errors and gaps generated because of the above-stated understanding gaps and because of changes in business environments between the time data was collected and the time implementation is completed.

On top of these:

- Consultants also make mistakes.
- When consultants become lead figures in a task, management tends to drop its guard, reducing controls and sanity checks.

In any case, management will be held responsible for consultants' mistakes, so why not pay for one's own?

There is no real alternative to good management. A consultant-led general cost reduction rarely succeeds as planned because consultants do not know the intangibles, crucial details, or trade secrets that make the company.

The use of consultants should be under a clear understanding of mutual expectations, tasks to be fulfilled, and deliverables.

Sales

Another example of delegation of incompetence occurs in sales partnerships. Many companies seek to accelerate expansion of their sales network. In an attempt to save money, management seeks to delegate the company's sales to a larger company (i.e. seeks to partner with a large company, which sells the company's product for them). Unless a very unique product or offering is involved, this will not work well. This is because a) the large company will focus on its own products, b) it takes time to educate sales forces on new offerings and markets, and c) salespeople will seek to maximize their commissions by selling known and accepted products.

Sememe sought for many years to develop sales partnerships. Management assumed that new partnerships would accelerate company growth and provide much-needed cash. Over the years, Sememe signed several cooperation agreements with major corporations worldwide. All of them failed. One company could not convince the salespeople to offer the product because they were stuck to their comfort zones. Another company lost interest after realizing that the sales effort was bigger than anticipated. In a third company, the sales mentor resigned. In the fourth company, the internal mentor passed away.

(Once the mentor within a big company leaves or is unsuccessful in growing sales, that potential partner is lost. The time and cost to develop a new partnership are prohibitive for small and medium companies.)

When Sememe's management tried to delegate its incompetence—its inability to sell and create sales—it failed for three central reasons:

First, no substantial sales were generated because company energies were funneled into strategic partnerships rather than into the generation of sales.

Second, by not trying hard enough to sell, the company couldn't prove its offering was good and had a large enough market attraction to be interesting to a large company.

Third, low sales showed that management did not believe in its own ability to sell and was trying to avoid the tedious work involved in generating sales.

These two errors cost the company time and money.

Subsequently, as part of the turnaround process that I devised and led, sales efforts were shifted to developing a worldwide distributor network. We motivated salespeople by increasing commissions and strengthening customer support. Within two years, sales almost tripled and profits soared.

Forms of Speech

Another form of incompetence delegation arises through unfocused communications. When people phrase things in overly complicated ways, they force listeners or readers to unravel their meaning. This invariably wastes time and often leads to misunderstandings and accusations.

Resist the urge to over-explain. If you want to explain something, imagine you're explaining it to a child. Keep your words simple and your sentences short. If you're writing something, keep it concise and clear. You'll not only aid your reader's understanding; you'll aid your own as well.

Do not delegate your inability to sharpen your thoughts and express them in a simple and comprehensible form. Listeners are burdened with their activities and will not spend time trying to decipher the message you are trying to convey.

As Albert Einstein put it: "If you can't explain it simply, you don't understand it well enough."

Upward Delegation

Upward delegation is also typical of incompetence. It reflects on both the delegating and the receiving parties. Many subordinates find creative ways to rid themselves of work by either returning it to their superiors or delegating it sideways to peers. Sweet-talking unaware people into accepting additional work is a social art.

Superiors sometimes find themselves doing their subordinates' work without meaning to. Upward delegation may be, for example, due to deadlines or because "it's faster if I do it myself than explain again" attitudes. Subordinate incompetence may be caused by anything from laziness to ignorance.

Upward delegation rarely happens in healthy organizations—in which managers also act as mentors, helping employees execute their tasks.

Indecision

Indecision is a known and costly way to avoid responsibility. Many un-deciders, non-deciders, and people who decide not to decide delegate their decision-making responsibilities. Sometimes, they delegate to their superiors, sometimes to a committee or other type of group or to a consultant. A group decision is marked by the fact that no one is really responsible for the decision or its controls, improvement, or results.

Another symptom of indecision is the addiction to supporting information. As supporting information keeps flowing in because of changes in environments, needs, technologies, competition, and markets, non-deciders use it as a pretext to continuously postpone decisions.

Decisions have to be made. Decisions are about calculated risks. Smart decisions normally follow preparation and accumulated experience. These should be made, executed, and controlled all the way through. Thus, an important objective of corporate executives is to delegate decision making to competent people.

Decisions should be judged according to the environment, information, and tools available at the time the decisions are made. It is easy to criticize decisions once actions become history. It is harder to make them in real time, when an actual decision should be made. Post-factum criticism is justified only when it is constructive, as part of self- and internal improvement processes. Otherwise, unless major issues were overlooked, post-factum criticism is useless. Chances are, given the same set of circumstances, the critics would have also failed.

In spite of the aforesaid, many decisions do turn out to be bad ones because of egos or fears. Ego translates to attitudes such as "I know it all," "I cannot degrade myself by asking," or "Don't confuse my mind with facts! It's already made up." Fear translates into not admitting weakness and not expressing thoughts such as "I don't really know" or "I am embarrassed to ask."

Fear translates into indecision; haste translates into mistakes.

To support decisions, encourage open discussions, brainstorming, and productive disagreements. A good manager will create disagreements if there are none, then, once a decision is made, stick to it; no need to tweak it as execution develops. A good decision is independent of execution details. Instead, it depends on crucial details that remain as anchors throughout the review process, if properly identified and analyzed.

Here again, the ability to intelligently stick to decisions is a matter of personality—the ability to see the big picture and accept risks. Every project, activity, or company experience reaches times in which even good managements doubt the correctness of its decisions.

In Greek mythology, King Sisyphus was doomed to eternally roll a boulder up a hill, only to watch it roll back down, over and over again. Sometimes, management feels the same way—that it's working hard and doing all the right things but never advancing. Pressure mounts high, doubts arise, and sleep is lost. Should decisions be reviewed? Should the ship's course be changed? If you, the decision maker, have done your work properly, carefully looking at all angles and aspects, then believe in yourself. Alternative decisions will not necessarily be better, but they will surely require additional time and money.

Chapter 9:
Execution

Execution is about *who does what, how, and when.* Leadership defines the *who,* grand strategy defines the *what,* and execution strategy defines the *how* and *when.* These terms are discussed in detail in Chapter 3.

Organizational Structure

Historically, centralistic management structures were applied. Decisions were made at the top by three to five executives who were allowed to think while the rest of the employees had to execute. This managerial structure develops corporate bureaucracy, which results in slow and time-consuming processes. Bureaucracy is sometimes fittingly depicted in the phrase "A camel is a horse designed by a committee."

In today's competitive and information-saturated world, a world in which product lifecycles are sometimes as short as two years, decision and execution must be prompt. In order to be dynamic, companies use a distributed management structure. In this structure, hierarchies are flat and managers have substantial responsibility and authority—and thus must be high caliber in terms of leadership, vision, and sales or technology. The overall cost of mistakes in distributed management companies is still lower than the cost of bureaucracy in centrally managed companies.

Cisco and Motorola are examples of each of the above structures—or, rather, attitudes. In the 1990s, while Cisco developed a distributed and agile structure with top business results, Motorola remained with its historically centralistic management style. Motorola's slow-moving structure jeopardized the company during the last decade of the second millennium and first decade of the third millennium. The company was unable to adapt itself quickly enough to the changing business environment and thus lost market share and cash reserves.

Execution Strategy

Execution strategy refers to the *when* and *how* of a company—that is, the daily tools and activities that converge into results as defined by the grand strategy. Execution strategy is as crucial to success as grand strategy is.

Execution strategies may include such aspects as:

- How to design software support to ensure continuity of share trading.
- Manufacturing concepts to maximize production output.
- Choosing agricultural tools for best crop yields.
- Choosing R&D development platforms.

When planning an execution strategy, creative, out-of-the-box thinking can reveal powerful shortcuts. A wonderful example from nature is water—the most frequent rock breaker. Water, which does not compress, penetrates small cracks in rocks. When the rock heats and expands, it attempts to compress the water, ending in the rock breaking because the water won't yield to its pressure. Alternatively, when water cools and passes the anomaly temperature, it expands, leading to breakage once again. Managers should actively seek cracks in rocks to create corporate and product excellence.

Seeking cracks encompasses many issues. Regardless of topic, however, information is a necessity, and the scope of discussion should be widened to include relevant disciplines and information about the ecosystem of the company and its products, as well as the ecosystem in which the company operates. Possible future events, their potential impact, and their viability over time are just some considerations. As with any decision making, it's important to break out of old comfort zones and habits, proactively look for innovative angles, and learn through studying more and wider-radius information.

Debate is helpful for seeking out the flaws in ideas. In any brainstorming session, there should be at least one person playing devil's advocate. This person should be appointed to look for the negative implications of every positive aspect of a plan—a sort of yin-and-yang technique.

Once the downsides of a plan are understood, a decision is made considering whether those downsides can be controlled and lived with. In physics, inefficiencies are reflected as heat; in business, they are reflected as cost. We learn to live with both.

Leadership and Management

Leadership is about inspiring people to follow your ideas and your path, but inspiration alone is not enough. To efficiently achieve results, one needs:

- Structure
- Delegation of authority and responsibility
- Planning and execution
- Controls and feedbacks

The Mandarins, Romans, and Incas all had great administrative and management skills and they understood their value in the running of an empire. Without great vision, administration, and management, the Incas could not have built 18,000 miles of roads and 2,000 waystations in their almost-2,500-mile-long empire. But they did, and those roads enabled them to develop social structures, trading and tax collection systems, and other elements that let the rulers support their subjects while enforcing their rule. Simply put, management and administration are essential elements in the application of leadership.

Most people like to be led and expect to be told what to do. Sure, they complain about it—but they need it. People need frameworks and structures, instructions and plans, personal interaction, and other agendas to dictate their daily lives. Being controlled by established routines gives us humans a sense of security and stability. Leadership uses management and administration to apply these, giving people the comfort they seek. This perceived comfort is accompanied by upsides like "freedom." After the Glasnost, many elder Russians missed the perceived safety and clear rules of communism. Nowadays, freedom seems to mean being enslaved by consumerism and taxation.

Modern government, or what we refer to as Western democracy, is structured in a similar way. Leadership changes while management, administration, and structure remain. Most of the laws enacted are *don't-do* or *must-do* laws. A far smaller portion of the laws are positive laws concerning citizen rights and what citizens are entitled to receive from the state or have the right to do. This is not a coincidence; it is a reflection of human nature. Much like governments, corporations have structures, rules, and procedures that impose on employees work processes in an attempt to ensure consistent operation.

A simple example of poor leadership is what happens when the boss walks into the room and suddenly everybody pretends to be busy; when he steps back out, employees release a sigh of relaxation and chatter resumes.

To be good, leadership has to send a message of trust, such as: "Yes, I know you are chatting, and that is okay as long as the work gets done." This approach is the reverse of the controlling micromanager who wants to see everybody producing all the time. Both approaches have advantages and disadvantages. Trust may lead to disappointments, while micromanagement results in inefficiency and lack of motivation. Leadership is about the balance point between management and people-driven results, between imposing on employees and exposing talent. Leadership is about providing the positive drive needed to improve a company.

Personalities

There are many types of leaders and managers, but not many people are good at both leading and managing. While management is about execution, leadership is about vision and its implementation. Management is normally delegated to key followers with managerial skills or other relevant abilities.

In rough terms, we identify three types of managers:

- Generalists with broad horizons who understand the big picture.

- Detail-oriented people.

- Combinations of both—people who understand the big picture and are able to identify the critical details that keep the big picture alive.

It is fair to say that while we are born with certain abilities, we are able to improve, within limits, our basic talents through practice.

Generalists. These people have broad horizons and the ability to see the big picture and understand the big system. As such, they are normally visionaries. They are dreamers with a talent to connect remote points of the grand scheme. They are normally verbal and charismatic but have a hard time bringing structure into their visions or executing them. To generate success, visionaries seek enthusiastic followers to grow into strong managers.

Detail-oriented people. Being detail-oriented is not necessarily a limitation or glass ceiling, because details can be essential in bringing a vision to life. However, detail-oriented people are easily lost when the big picture is concerned and too many interactions are involved. This sometimes causes them to dig in their heels. Detail-oriented people have to be carefully supervised by generalists or combinations, but can deliver good results when the nature of their work leverages their strengths.

You can tell if a person is detail oriented by the way he or she expresses ideas. Detail-oriented people are normally dealing with a crisis of some sort, or they'll always have something coming up and requiring their attention. Even on vacation, at night, during lunch, or at dinner, detail-oriented people are busy micromanaging. This makes them feel needed, important, and in control, and it boosts their self-esteem. When properly managed, detail-oriented people can excel and make substantial contributions to the company's success.

Combinations of both. The third type comprises people with both a broad system overview and an eye for detail. These people understand strategy and the big picture but can also identify details crucial for success. They take the big picture and convert it into a workable process. They structure and staff the organization to execute the tasks that make the vision come true. They seek out details crucial for vision implementation while disregarding technical details that can be implemented one way or another. Normally, these managers, in spite of being very busy, have time to listen because they learn from every bit of information that comes their way and because they delegate with well-defined expected outcomes.

It is the job of leaders to make sure they place each of these management types in positions best suited for their talents. A mix of talents is needed and should be applied and driven correctly to maximize results and returns. A strong leader will also recognize his or her own shortcomings and compensate for them through choice of the right team members. One good way to create balance in thinking, planning, execution, and control is to be aware of your own type and then hire your complementary opposites.

Priorities

Management sets execution priorities, intervenes when necessary, and works closely with teams verifying seamless transition when implementing changes in, for example: products, processes, flow, or company mergers.

Managers should be where growth or change is generated and where problems need to be solved. In healthy companies, efforts should focus on growth; in distressed companies, efforts should focus on problem solving and growth generation.

Let's take a brief look at project launches, which are growth-oriented activities that require careful prioritization.

Projects are launched with all required resources: human, budget, knowhow, and management. The feeling is good and time seems abundant, leading to the adoption of laidback or bureaucratic attitudes.

Meetings, reviews, and discussions take place, giving management a sense of control. As time progresses, small delays start accumulating, affecting the project's critical path.

The "administrators" fail to identify the problem and its cumulative impact on success. The impact of daily activities on releasing slow-building bottlenecks is overlooked, resulting in loss of time, money, and client credibility.

Problems are inevitable, but they don't have to result in crashed projects. Preventing such long-term, slowly building problems is easy: simply increase the time pressure at the beginning of a project instead of at the end, because at the beginning of a project, all resources are available and all variables can be affected like the early purchase of long lead-time items, handling legal and regulatory issues from day one, setting proper priorities, and carefully planning how to handle interfaces. As more thought and action are exercised at the beginning, more potential problems surface and solutions are generated. This reduces the "expected unexpected" (the known-to-come unexpected problems).

Think of a project like building a house. Detailed planning, parallel work, and timeline optimization can help to ensure the shortest possible construction time. Once plans are in place and execution begins, we will continuously verify timely material delivery—not assume it will arrive on time. We verify that a subcontractor's work complies with relevant standards; we notify suppliers as early as possible of any schedule changes, helping them make the best use of their resources and gaining their trust.

It is here that start-up companies can create their success. Comprehensive high-level and interface planning will help identify pitfalls, risks, and the like. The better the analysis, the higher the success probability is. The planning process may also lead entrepreneurs to the honest conclusion that their good idea is not as good as they thought or cannot meet market requirements. If planning reveals critical flaws, goals should be changed; don't wave the problems away. Throughout this process, managerial and leadership skills affect the breadth, depth, and integrity of such analysis.

The next step is priority setting, a skill that requires a holistic view of the goals and resources at hand, the ability to break those goals down into executable tasks, and a healthy level of investigative willpower. Priority setting also requires managers to withstand pressures from team members who oppose the priorities set because these whoreduce their participation or shift resources away from them.

Decisions

The motto of fearless management is: "Managers should be praised for correct decisions, reprimanded for bad decisions, but never be blamed for indecision."

Indecision is a costly mistake. It results in fixed costs spent without any return, idling people, low motivation, and lack of direction. It is a ship without sails whose captain fell asleep. Making and executing a bad decision sets a baseline, a reference line for correction and eventual convergence to a positive path. Although wrong decisions are also costly, they're normally less costly than indecision and idling. From wrong decisions a lesson is learned, from idling none.

Decisions are about choosing between alternatives. If there seem to be no alternatives, it's the manager's duty to create more because decisions are made between alternatives. Teams can help with this—in fact, they should, because creating alternatives drives teamwork and corporate creativity.

Once a decision is made, make sure you communicate it clearly to your team and stick with it. Unless a major flaw surfaces, don't let doubts and fears drag you into slowdowns and indecision.

Chapter 10:
Selling

Selling is an art. It is a human art, a hunt to be enjoyed. Humans sell to humans. If a potential client has a bad gut feeling about a salesperson or a sales website, he or she probably will not buy anything, even the best of products. The buyer's gut feeling will keep him or her asking, "Where's the catch?" The art of selling is a qualitative art succeeded by quantitative elements like specifications, legal terms, pricing, and deal conclusion.

Salespeople, as referred to in this section, include all employees who interface with company-related people, including clients, shareholders, suppliers, and bankers. The sales process is different with each, but all salespeople are selling something—products, images, branding, pride, financial stability, and even themselves. Company salespeople span from shareholders and executives downwards.

Communication skills are crucial for salespeople—not only in terms of expressing themselves, but also in terms of listening. Listen to clients, sense them, and understand their needs or the problems they seek to solve. Solve client problems, and you have solved yours. They buy, and you sell; this is a win-win situation. In some instances, the problem might be the mere desire for the joy of buying an unnecessary consumer product. In others, it might be a large, specialized project. Be close to clients and listen to them carefully as you solve their problems and help them fulfill their wishes. Listen carefully; watch their body language so you can sense what remains unsaid.

"I don't have the product you want, but what about this [other] one?" This is a typical response of a poor salesperson. This approach may work in the case of emotional purchasing decisions like presents, clothing and accessories, even furniture and cars. But it is not the right approach in the professional world.

Most professional clients know what they want and what goals they want to achieve with it. Professional clients who do not know what the right solution is are mostly able to describe the problem they want to have solved. Knowingly or not, clients imply where stumbling blocks are—be those knowhow, infrastructure, access to financing or resources, or something else. A good salesperson will use his or her knowhow to identify opportunities through the unspoken or unmentioned subjects. Listen to what is *not* said—come prepared and understand the wider implication of the issue at hand. Identification of client oversights or lack of knowledge may reveal a business opportunity that, picked by a good salesperson, will be turned into a sale.

When offering a solution to a client, address the client's problem together with its indirect implications or side effects. Giving clients a comprehensive solution makes them feel that you understand not only their direct needs but also the environment in which they operate. A few weeks after a client granted us a contract, he asked me, "Do you know why we granted you the contract?

Because we felt you *understand* what we want." And we did. Understanding is the intangible part of sales, the personal and professional trust that is the foundation on which sales transactions are based.

Patience, within limits, is an asset. Unless one is very lucky, complex business deals will not occur overnight. Business deals have to be properly structured; from the first presentation to closing the deal, client and supplier have to be comfortable with the terms of the deal and the people involved. Sometimes adaptation to specific situations and personalities, tailored solutions, and a deal-specific approach are required. Properly planned and executed sales strategies will be rewarded by clients.

The Walkman

As discussed earlier, many companies that listened to their clients tailored solutions that revolutionized industries. That said, the opposite has also occurred. In the 1970s, Akio Morita, SONY's legendary founder and chairman, sought ways to make a portable, lightweight means for consumers to listen to their favorite music. He came up with the cassette tape Walkman. When the Walkman was introduced to consumer focus groups and marketing experts, they rejected the idea, stating a variety of reasons. Most reasons given reflected habits and comfort zones rather than forward thinking. In spite of the discouraging feedback, Morita decided to bring the product to the market and let the market decide. The Walkman[8] became an instant success, proving once again Morita's forward thinking.

---

8   It was succeeded by the Discman and, in a sense, by the iPod.

Make Clients Remember You

Happy and trusting clients are more cooperative. Make them positively remember the sales experience and the salesperson. Make them laugh; make them happy. Telling a good and timely joke or even spilling coffee might help. Yes, in the short term, spilling coffee might make you look clumsy, but over time, clients will remember you without remembering why. They might separately remember the clumsy man or woman who spilled the coffee, but it's rare that the person and the act will be remembered in conjunction. The risk is not big while returns may be.

Ensure that in every phone call or interaction, the client is exposed to new information. This makes the salesperson interesting. It makes clients willing to accept his or her calls, as there are always novelties. Salespeople have to avoid repeating themselves or they'll bore their clients.

It is a great feeling, probably mutual, when a client remembers the salesperson. This is especially true if no recent communications or business transactions took place. The worst case for a salesperson is having a majority of clients who remember neither him nor his company. On top of being insulting, it points to a lack of sales skills.

The Domino Effect

The domino effect is all around us. We are immersed in it. One thing occurs, and it triggers another action that causes another event, creating a chain effect. In the case of business, the domino effect is exploited through branding and is reflected by social *me-too* pressures:

A uses X.

B sees A using X.

B decides to use X.

C and D see A and B using X.

C and D start using X.

Companies lacking financial resources to pay for expensive branding, but wishing to expand and grow, benefit from this domino effect. If you're interested in learning more about this, check out the 1841 book *Extraordinary Popular Delusions and the Madness of Crowds* by Charles MacKay.

Domino effects can be created to target specific markets without the burden of high costs. Domino effects are applied mostly in predefined communities, creating interest in a product or service. It is what social networks do.

In Sememe, I decided to increase export sales. The product and its benefits had limited exposure in its targeted countries. Therefore, I devised the domino plan based on my experience being on the receiving end of the domino effect:

Professional or industrial products have a limited number of key clients in each country for each product line. When a new representative or distributor is considering distributing a product line, he will first approach the key clients to receive their professional opinion on the product and its company.

When the first distribution company approached the key clients, it received positive opinions. Better still, when the second distributor approached the same key clients, it heard a positive remark in the form of: "Yes, I already heard of the product." And so on.

Distributors want to be identified with known products in the same way people seek to be identified with celebrities by name dropping. The fact that key clients had heard of the product motivated distributors to represent us and sell our products. The domino effect was in motion; Sememe successfully created a focused local-branding. It worked to the point that, in one country, two potential representatives fought each other to represent the distressed company Sememe!

How to Kill a Business and Have the Client Love You

Client-supplier relationships should be clear of negativism. Think of the Japanese, who develop relationships despite a non-confrontational attitude and avoiding the use of the word *no*.

There are many creative ways to circumvent the bad taste of a negative answer. The trick is to use a positive-no language.

For example, if you offer the best prices on the market but unacceptable delivery times, you won't make a sale. However, if you clarify that the reason delivery times are so long is "factory overload," then you leave the client with a positive impression: "Their product is so amazing that it's in high demand!"

Likewise, if you offer an over-featured product at a higher-than-market price, you likely won't make a sale. However, if you clarify that it's more expensive because of "unique high-level features," then you leave the client with a positive impression: "Their product is much more advanced than the other products. It is the future, and therefore justifies its high price." This is the case with today's smartphones, for example.

You won't make a sale either way—the positive no is, after all, a way of saying "no"—but you will leave the client feeling good about you and therefore open to possible future deals.

The Offering

In our era of information inundation, products and services should have sufficiently notable differentiators to support almost instant decisions. Differentiators have to be clearly communicated and highlighted. In consumer goods, differentiators may be qualitative aspects— like aesthetics, branding, or image. In technology, differentiators are about features and performance. In industry, they are return on investment. In commodities, they are quality and supply. In all cases, price performance, cost effectiveness, and perceived value versus price are all or part of the deciding factors.

Creativity is key to increase sales. It may be triggered by many factors, such as identifying market trends, integrating more product features, development teams thinking out of the box, product managers identifying opportunities, interviewing people and clients, and so on. For example, years ago a friend of mine returned from Southeast Asia with simple, cheap, yet colorful necklaces. He tried to sell them, but no one was willing to buy this "cheap" stuff. He quadrupled the price, and all the necklaces were sold in no time.

Of the ideas that come up, look for the lowest-hanging fruit: namely, the easiest achievable growth factor. Normally, this includes the most accessible markets, existing technologies and materials, lowest time to market, and highest profitability.

There is no magic. Listen carefully to clients, to what they say and what they don't say, and then apply your conclusions in a creative, intensive, and hardworking manner. Gain a time advantage over competition, which is probably working on similar ideas.

Service as a Business Driver

Service is a major business driver. Service builds long-term trust between clients and suppliers, and between suppliers and their representatives. Service is about listening to clients and their frustrations. Send people overseas to solve problems, replace defective products, and help quantify and solve client problems.

Prompt service is a way to clarify misunderstandings. Problems need to be quantified and solved as early as possible. Delaying solutions to gain short-term financial savings will result in the loss of clients and credibility, and higher overall cost. Client retention costs less than client acquisition. Here again, a stitch in time saves nine. Or as restaurant owner put it: "You liked the food—tell your friends; you didn't like it—tell us."

A manufacturer of emergency lighting equipment won a tender to supply its equipment to a mall under construction. After installing the equipment, the electrical contractor complained that most units did not work due to quality problems. As time was of the essence, pressures mounted, voices were raised, payments withheld, arguments became emotional, and facts were forgotten altogether. Finally, one of the engineers made a qualitative decision to quantify the problem by sending a technician to inspect the over-1000 installed units. The results provided a corrective experience, practically solving the dispute in no time. It turned out that except for four failed units, the rest were incorrectly installed. Emotions vanished into thin air.

Chapter 11:
Market Reports and Forecasts

Business plans are about how to achieve business goals with the ultimate goal of achieving a specific share of a defined market. For the purpose of assessing the business opportunity and anchor business-plan financials, most companies use market forecasts.

Market forecasts provide the size and projected direction of the total available market for a product group. Forecasts do not necessarily indicate how much of the market is accessible to the Company's specific products. Unless the company is a monopoly, only estimates of future market share and sales growth can be made.

When a company seeks to dramatically grow sales, beyond natural market growth, it is trying to grow on account of competitors' market share. This is a challenging goal requiring creativity and excellence—both being qualitative, people-driven parameters.

Market reports, including projections and forecasts, mostly provide extrapolated trends mirroring supplier expectations. Such forecasts cannot foresee market dips or sudden shifts. In addition, actual sales depend on a company's ability to reach a specific person in a given organization or household and convince her or him to buy a specific product or service. Market studies do not provide names and contacts of real buyers, thus requiring an additional penetration effort.

In the early 1990s, American corporations spent approximately two billion dollars on consumer goods market research, surveys, and focus groups from which forecasts and product opportunities were derived. During that same year, Japanese companies spent approximately one tenth of this sum, opting to invest the remainder of their money in making the product, bringing it to the market, and letting the market decide. This approach created huge savings in time and marketing costs, resulting in earlier sales growth of successful products. Advantages of the Japanese approach include identification of actual clients and the ability to bring ideas to markets more quickly, avoiding delays that give competition an edge.

The Japanese approach is valid where R&D investments are in the range of market survey cost or lower. For high-value, low-volume products like car chassis, robots, and airplanes, the market is limited by definition; thus, the small number of potential clients eases direct interviews with them. Normally, such clients are cooperative and glad to provide information about their needs and in return receive firsthand information as to future trends, performance, features, pricing, and client benefits.

Optimism and Forecasts

Market reports are optimistic especially when the economy is growing. In shrinking economies, forecasts are very hard to make and furthermore to sell because no one wants to buy surveys that show shrinking markets or insinuate that industries will disappear because of emerging alternatives.

Managements prefer to buy positive news, not spend money on bad ones.

In 2005, Professor Nouriel Roubini warned that "home prices were riding a speculative wave that would soon sink the economy."[9] He predicted bad news for which there was no real demand until the subprime mortgage market collapsed. That event turned him into an oracle.

Similarly, Mark Thornton explains,[10] regarding the burst of the Dot-com:

> Two of the most famous predictions concerning the stock market came from James K. Glassman and Kevin A. Hassett (1999), who predicted at the apex of the stock-market bubble that the Dow Jones Industrial average would go up to 36,000, and from Robert J. Shiller (2000), who wrote at the same time that the stock market was suffering from "irrational exuberance," a phrase coined by Fed chairman Alan Greenspan.

Party spoilers. The stock market crash of 2000–2002 caused the loss of $5 trillion in the market value of companies from March 2000 to October 2002.[11]

But good managements leverage bad news to strengthen or save companies by refocusing, changing, and adapting. Failure results from managements and investors avoiding reality, overstretching resources, or not preparing for the unexpected. Once again, the decision

---

9 Nouriel Roubini, "8 who saw the crisis coming...," *Fortune*, Aug. 2008.

10 Mark Thornton. "Who Predicted The Bubble? Who Predicted The Crash?", The Independent Review, Volume IX, Number 1, Summer 2004.

11 Gaither, Chris; Chmielewski, Dawn C. (July 16, 2006). "Fears of Dot-Com Crash, Version 2.0". Los Angeles Times. Retrieved March 9, 2013.

about whether the company should prepare itself for a future slower economy is a qualitative one.

Another anomaly is that during market growth periods, all extrapolation methods predict growth. There is no mathematical model that will take a growth path and predict contraction. Therefore, contraction [negative growth] predictions are rarely found. Similarly, infinite growth is impossible because market growth must have at least periodical corrections, which market forecasting companies can rarely identify

Markets are affected by expectations, geopolitical events, and other macro factors that are impossible to integrate into market-specific surveys and resulting forecasts. Therefore, market reports, surveys, and forecasts must be independently assessed by the reader and used as one of several data sources. In some cases, careful reading of the body of the forecast reveals that the details do not fully support the conclusions.

Examples of Missed Sanity Checks

The following examples show the importance of qualitative thinking, expanding horizons, and forming independent opinions on matters at hand. Critical analysis of prior decisions, including one's own, helps generate improvement. The broader our horizons and the better our ability to critically and qualitatively analyze the big picture, the higher our probability of success.

For example, a careful observation of how projections are used when translating a strategy or vision into numbers shows a human tendency to treat projections as anchors, almost facts. These numbers cuddle us and make us look good when presenting plans. But when results fail to meet planning, our poor performance is exposed.

Market Forecast Disinformation

During the bubble years (prior to 2001), the authors of a market report I read stated that they'd interviewed industry experts whose names and telephone numbers were provided. I called two of them to discuss the statements quoted on their behalf. To my utter surprise, both said that not only had they not been interviewed, but that the views quoted on their behalf were not their views. The survey editors had simply wanted to give credibility to their "findings" not expecting anyone to check their sources.

Stuck with Business Plan and Losses

Another example of such cuddling is business plans that always show growth and eventual profits. A large US corporation decided to start its European subsidiary in Germany. The business plan showed eventual profits. After five years and yearly business plan updates, the subsidiary was still losing money. When a new CEO revised past business plans and compared them with actual results, he realized that the European subsidiary couldn't be profitable and shut it down. The former CEO could have done the same but was either caught up in inertia, under pressure from a subordinate, or unable to admit his mistaken decision to keep the subsidiary alive.

Subprime Demise

In August 2007, when Ben Bernanke, Chairman of the US Federal Reserve, announced that the central bank would increase market liquidity and cash facilities to commercial banks, many independent thinkers sold all their stocks and shares. I sold most, and I regret not selling all. One does not need to be a great economist to figure out that lack of banking liquidity means that something went wrong in financial markets. Banks are not supposed to require government extraordinary liquidity support. Yet most investors trusted the positive market trend to continue, embracing the comfort of numbers and trusting market makers to take care of them.

The 2007 subprime bubble resulted from mortgage-backed junk bonds at the base of the bond pyramid being bundled into AAA bonds at the top of the pyramid. It was a Ponzi scheme of which many industry players knew but chose to remain silent, while those who did stand up were looked upon as party spoilers. Few took the time to follow the tedious food chain of what exactly a specific bond or fund invests in.

Blind to the Big Picture

A technology company example is of a company I managed that, prior to my arrival (in 2000), invested five hundred thousand dollars in market surveys, two of which were from world-leading market research companies. All reports, five in total, predicted the sky for xDSL (internet) infrastructure equipment. As the CEO, I was concerned and decided to crosscheck the information. I found and read market forecasts of all components, products, and users in our vertical food chain, starting with the chip manufacturers producing the core xDSL chips. The chips were put into systems or subsystems by companies like ours, who sold their units to telephony companies and service providers. Service providers installed the xDSL units as part of their service deployment in offices and residences.

While the "xDSL box" market survey was very optimistic, reading the surveys for chips, telephone companies, and users revealed something shocking: for every five xDSL chips produced, only one was installed at an end-user location. When I called the respective market survey companies and asked them to verify or refute my findings, their first reaction was, "Impossible!" Their second reaction, two weeks later, was, "The oversupply conclusion is correct." My qualitative decision to look at the broad picture became an information enabler on which we successfully acted.

Those were the 1990s bubble years in which marketers, forecasters, and managements were busy shooting arrows and then drawing target circles around them. No sanity checks, no what-ifs; just pure self-convincing. A mass combination of wishful thinking and a gross disregard for the boundary problem took place. Some of the "offenders" were dreamers, while others were hoping to enjoy other people's money.

The forecasters' flaw resulted from having each of the product groups covered by different analysts, who failed to coordinate and verify the consistency and internal logic of the whole picture. This failure is a typical symptom of an interface problem (see Chapter 4 on The Boundary Problem). A huge number of company managements and investors trusted the forecast and used it as an anchor for their business plans, eventually finding themselves in financial trouble or disappearing altogether. Based on such reports, billions of investment dollars were raised and lost in one of the biggest shifts of wealth in American history.

The decision to make a high-level sanity check is a qualitative decision led by one's ability to think beyond the entity called "the company." It is the ability to look at the surrounding habitat and the company's place in it. Forming one's own opinion is essential, especially given market-survey companies' natural optimism.

Historical Perspective

Not all revolutions are quick to be embraced by industry leaders. Examples of this include Xerox photocopiers, personal computers, and hospital sterilization. In all three cases, experts, market surveys, and focus groups predicted failure. The persistence of visionaries is what proved them wrong.

Market surveys and forecasts, like company financials, are historical documents from which data extrapolation takes place in an attempt to predict the future. The main information sources for market forecasts are interviews with industrialists combined with top-down quantitative assessments. By the time interview coordination, data collection, analysis, report writing, publishing, and selling are concluded, the information is at least six months old. In addition, surveys are rarely in a position to foresee emerging or disruptive products that will conquer markets. Executives do not disclose to surveyors plans for new products let alone revolutionary ones, and existing products or markets do not point at such future innovation.

Another aspect of market reports is their tendency to handle specific, well-defined disciplines or market segments while avoiding the complexity of cross-discipline alternatives and the role of product families in users' food chains.

Lesson Learned

In many—perhaps most—cases, market surveys supply comfort to decision makers; however, over-reliance on market surveys is risky. Use surveys and forecasts with care, verify the findings with your clients, and listen to them carefully, to what they say and also to what they don't say. There is a lot of hidden information in what clients do not say, all the way from over-optimism to lack of market understanding. After all, most market surveys and forecasts are based on a) discussions with either suppliers or clients, and b) a comparison with historical data and trends. Talk to clients; get the same information as the analyst did; add the numbers; and, while doing so, win over clients.

As market information is the core of business plans, it must be continuously verified using a reasonable dosage of paranoia. Information can be verified by those individuals interfacing with clients—from the CEO down to back-office sales assistants. Communications with clients through verbal discussions rather than written exchanges can be goldmines.

Use verbal exchanges to discuss ideas, raise alternatives, and stimulate thinking, leading to new angles and business opportunities. However, as important as information is, one should not get addicted to collecting it.

Visit your clients and suppliers, especially those who also supply to competition. Visit tradeshows where mingling and networking takes place; pick up pieces of information; integrate and draw conclusions. Use your common sense and sensitivities. Communicate directly with clients and form your own opinion of the market.

Chapter 12:
Management and Innovation

Innovation means *making changes in something established, especially by introducing new methods, ideas, or products.*[12] Innovation stems from prior inventions. Innovation is the result of needs and shifts in habits that are part of human evolution. Over the past century, markets and products have expanded their innovation, introducing more complex products, new sales support activities, and terms like "client retention."

Innovation

Man's dream is to invent—or at least to come up with high-impact innovations.

Both invention and innovation require a certain level of chaos, chaotic thinking, and random movement. Inventions and innovations rarely emerge in systematic and over-structured environments. It is not a coincidence that true scientific and industrial innovation comes from open societies that allow thinking and criticism. The pluralistic ways of such societies allow a multitude of ideas

---

12   Oxford Dictionary

to be cultivated and tested. The US and Israel are two such examples.

As invention opportunities are rare, the world encounters mostly innovation—a complex issue by itself. Innovation spans a wide range of ideas, from simple, local, and easy-to-bypass innovations to truly disruptive ideas like Voice over IP.

Patent books are full of registered "inventions"— most of which are innovations, not inventions. Many are useless, short lived, or easy to circumvent. A fraction of the patents represent real progress—such as fluorescent lamps, telephony and radio, cars, the engine, plastics, and some drugs.

Company managers seek innovations with long-term impact and high barriers of entry that will make those innovations difficult for competitors to reproduce. Entry barriers are not always easy to generate; therefore, patents are registered to serve as such. A patented product is perceived as more advanced, though in most cases there is no substantial difference or innovation between a patented product and its patent-less counterpart. Management should seek small yet powerful tools that lead to big and lasting differentiators and changes.

Evolutionary challenges have led to innovation. New terms like enterprise resource planning (ERP), digital video (later: versatile) disc player (DVD), total quality management (TQM), VoIP, video on demand (VoD), and others have become standard terms and practices in our daily lives; and more continue to emerge. Management should lead its team to new ideas and be aware of new market opportunities, emerging technologies, and simpler ways of doing complex things. Know the world and expand horizons; break away from schematic thinking and generate "crazy" ideas. Review, check, and discuss all ideas to avoid missing a good one.

Evolution

Over the past two centuries, two interesting processes took place: the continuous exploitation and commercialization of technologies and products derived from basic research or inventions; and, secondly, an evolution in the drivers of sales.

During the past 200 years, mankind has made great leaps in the discovery, invention, and application of paradigm shifts that change the way we live our lives. Motors, airplanes, electricity, radios, new textile materials, penicillin, and computers are some examples of disciplines and products that evolved, and that have kept evolving over the past century. Each is based on disruptive, out-of-the-box thinking as well as the new ideas of creative and daring people. The pace of innovation is so fast that scientific invention can't keep up with industry demand.

The Evolution of What Drives Sales

This process has to do with the mass-application of ideas.

Technology era. Initially, technologies were scarce, and it required great skill and expense to create new technologies or make products incorporating them. Companies who had a better technology became market leaders.

Branding era. As technologies, methods, and knowhow became more accessible, barriers to entry lowered and competition increased. New differentiators were sought, shifting the world from technology driven to marketing and branding driven.

Quality era. Branding is expensive and was originally paid for by lowering quality (to clients' disappointment). The result was quality-aware clients seeking quality products and sustainable performance. And so the quality-focus years came to be, stressing issues like total quality management (TQM) to ensure product quality.

Service era. Quality in turn made products more expensive and, combined with the emergence of more sophisticated products, led to the service age. Product returns, technical support, immediate deliveries, and call centers became part of our daily lives stressing customer service and retention.

Integration era. As barriers to entry continued to drop and technologies became more mature and accessible, the integration era dawned. Integration of services meant such innovations as the bundling of telephone, internet, and TV services; one-stop shops where anything from yogurt to tires, TVs, and GPS systems are offered; and cars sold with integrated audio, video, GPS, and auto-reverse systems.

In short, the evolution process shifted consumers from technology to marketing to quality to service and now to integration and social-led product concepts. What is the next stage? Good question.

The above evolution process may not be valid for all disciplines, but the trend exists, driving competition and differentiation and affecting our daily lives.

Evolution requires innovation, which, in industry, is driven and fostered by managements that let people dream and then help them fulfill their dreams.

Thinking and Deciding

Innovation is about observing; thinking; analyzing; gathering information; and identifying knowhow, voids, and gaps. Innovation is also about free-floating thoughts and sparks of inspiration. Implementation of innovative ideas may be complex to develop and implement, requiring additional brainpower and resources.

Conversion of new ideas into corporate innovation is an intricate task, especially when the goal is products and sales. Corporate innovation has to consider commercial and financial aspects before investing in turning innovation into products. Product success also depends on its perceived value to buyers and on buyers' alternatives. It depends on end-product costs, manufacturing process and facilities, features, and capital investments that affect end-product price and its subsequent success.

Management, using its holistic view, should decide which innovation should reach the market. Management should listen to its innovators, product managers, salespeople, and logistics and manufacturing people. Listen to the thinking people who analyze the odds in their respective fields.

Managers are information integrators, those who collect information, filter it, structure it, and generate a full and coherent picture of opportunities and risks. The more the team thinks, analyzes, and plays devil's advocate, the better the chances of success. A thinking team is an asset—in spite of the complexity of managing ambitious, motivated, thinking, and opinionated people. Thinking is an ongoing process and discussion, not a time-framed meeting.

In spite of the aforesaid, non-corporate determined visionaries strive to materialize on their dreams, overlooking financial stress and accepting a huge personal burden on the way to success.

Sources of Innovation

Innovation in today's world is not an easy task. Innovation is no longer about improving what already exists; it is about invention, new methods of observation, and out-of-the-box thinking.

As mentioned, creativity requires a certain level of chaos combined with wide horizons. This is the out-of-the-box thinking that creates new realities, unexpected matches, and surprising combinations.

Every year, 3M awards its scientists $100,000 to research ideas for which "no sensible, conventional person in the company would give money."[13] Idea sparking can come from various sources, eventually developing into knowhow. Innovation flourishes when free thinking is stimulated and encouraged. Below are three methods that will help you develop business-viable innovation.

Innovation is relevant not only in R&D; it is applicable in sales, marketing, operations, and any other company activity. Though not all innovations will be applied, maintaining a level of creativity will help advance the company in the long term.

Be Close to Your Clients

As discussed, clients are a great source of inspiration, because they trigger innovation through need. Innovation may be cutting edge or simple; it may be discovered through targeted research work or through coincidence in a variety of technology platforms like chemicals, fibers, and oil.

Procter & Gamble has a *listen-to-the-client* policy based on which products are developed to meet specific market needs and tastes like colors, scents, pricing, and

---

13   "3M's Innovation Revival," *Fortune*, September 27th, 2010.

package sizes. Similarly, car manufacturers adapt their offering to end markets by stripping or adding features and changing engine sizes to meet local tastes and price targets. Global chocolate manufacturers adapt tastes, melting temperatures, and crunchiness to local tastes.

When starting a new development, ask yourself if the client—or if you—would be willing to pay for the product or service you intend to offer. Are the right differentiators being generated? Are enough differentiators being offered? Are you the only one in love with your idea, or will the public also fall in love with it? Does the new design or idea support future price-drop projections? Simulate the client, listen to him or her, immerse yourself in client thinking, and decide from that perspective.

Semikron, a German semiconductor company, listened to its client Siemens. Siemens needed a way to electrically isolate heat-generating electronic devices from their cooling platforms. Semikron came up with a creative idea called the "isolated base plate semiconductor housing." To ensure continuous product delivery, Siemens asked for a second source supplier that would supply the product in case Semikron couldn't.

Not only did Semikron give away the technology for free to a Japanese competitor, but they did not patent it because they thought the market was small and negligible. This revolutionary technology became the world standard, enabling shrinkage of electronic power supplies, motor drives, electric cars, and other power systems. Semikron listened to their client's needs and put their creativity to work. The result was a revolutionary, quickly adopted solution.

Daily business dealings also lead to innovations like overcoming barriers to entry, and creating user alternatives and ways to reduce costs. These and other business challenges can be leveraged as sources of innovation, of ideas that strengthen and improve product positioning compared to competition.

Listening to others is a great source of innovation.

Tinker and Play

An accumulation of past experience and knowhow is required to invent and generate the future. Out-of-the-box thinking and luck will not hurt. Tinker, play, be exposed to coincidence, and surprise yourself. Go for the unexpected, un-thought-of, and scientifically unproven ideas. Take care not to get stuck with scientists who defend what they know rather than research the unknown. Learn the 3M lesson.

Ideas arise out of inspiration, mental noises, and gut feelings. This is not to say that all such ideas are good ideas, but they may be surprising, eye opening, and interestingly simple. Patience and perseverance are important virtues in innovation.

The liquid-crystal display or LCD is based on research dating back to the 1888 work done by the Austrian botanist and chemist Friedrich Reinitzer. The technology matured in RCA laboratories in 1964 and was industrialized in the 1970s. Thus, when enjoying our laptops, cellphones, or televisions, we are enjoying over eighty years of accumulation and exploitation of scientific knowhow and additional decades of engineering advancement.

The semiconductor switch was first developed at AT&T Labs in 1947, winning its developers a Nobel Prize. The roots of this development go back to Michael Faraday's 1833 discovery of increasing electrical conduction with temperature in silver sulfide crystals. This disruptive technology revolutionized the world, enabling the eventual development of the first microprocessor and a myriad of semiconductor devices now used in almost every facet of our lives: in smart ID tags, credit cards, TVs, cell phones, laptops, white goods, cars, medical implants, and so on.

Brain Mining

Brain mining is about talking to people, asking questions, covering different angles, peeking into memory cells, tying together remote ideas, and integrating and verifying information using various sources.

Brain mining should include all sources of knowledge and information including clients, staff, competitors, users, suppliers, and laymen. The challenge is to probe further when loose ends are detected and identify the untapped opportunity.

The importance of brain mining for innovation purposes is not limited to product development. It includes sales, marketing, product management, operations, negotiations, networking—everything and anything that helps support corporate and personal growth.

The following experience illustrates the value of brain mining. A PhD friend of mine is a marine biologist specializing in on-shore growth of sea algae, also known as sea weeds. By growing algae in manmade pools, he increases the number of harvest cycles per year and controls the chemical composition of the algae through growth temperature and the chemical substances put into the water ponds. The result is consistency and higher and predictable yields. His methodology and process solves the industrialization barriers of sea-harvested algae.

After one failed commercialization attempt, my friend and his investors wondered what other uses they could develop for on-shore algae growth. The question was what.

He asked me to come, listen, and work with the team to identify the new opportunity. The initial business models were a no go, so I started asking questions, opening radiuses, climbing mountains, and exploring valleys to get a better feel for what in the algae composition is valuable for potential users. Being an ignoramus in marine biology (or any biology, for that matter), I had questions that were high level and focused on the applicative aspects of algae and their derivatives.

We reached the point where my scientific friend left the ideas he was stuck with and started "walking" with me. He started shifting his thinking away from science and chemistry to uses and applications. To his surprise, he found himself mentioning that a certain type of algae was the only source for agar, a compound used in medicine and biology with no synthetic alternative.

Now that he'd changed his thinking pattern, he also recalled reading of other applications for the extract. He went home and found out that there were some twenty possible major uses of the extract in consumer, professional, and medical markets that can total billions of dollars in yearly sales.

Algae chemical consistency and predictable availability are the key to serving said markets. No manufacturer can depend on the seasonality and variance of sea-harvested algae. My friend's technology enables the ongoing supply of quality algae, a disruptive solution.

Necessity is the Mother of Invention

Investing for a better future should be done hand in hand with practices dedicated to increase today's profitability and competitiveness. Salaries are a major expense in most companies. They should be set according to an employee's contribution to the company. Two weak employees will always be less effective and less efficient than one good employee.

A simple yet real-life cost-reduction example is this:

When I assumed the CEO's position at Sememe, I instructed all purchase orders to be signed off personally by me—including office supplies and cleaning materials. The effect was instantaneous and surprisingly impressive. Suddenly, employees had to justify all expenses. This made them think hard about whether they really needed what they asked for, if there were alternatives, and if they were willing to justify the expense to their superiors.

Employees started thinking creatively and finding alternatives and workarounds. One side effect was that for four months, no office supply requests were made, because staff used stocks piled in their drawers and cabinets. This was a deep educational process that helped ensure that funds were used to serve ROI-related needs.

Other cost-reduction changes I made included implementation of a well-known purchasing practice—shifting from batch manufacturing to yearly procurement contracts. This generated a 20% savings on parts purchasing. The new corporate attitude, combined with ongoing results, made employees realize that there were alternatives to most actions—including their behavior. It generated positive energies that improved teamwork and promoted eventual success.

Chapter 13:
Your Company

Know Your Company's Limitations

"Limitations" is a relative term. All companies have limitations that manifest themselves in comparison to competition, in the ability to achieve goals and be profitable, and so on. Corporate goals and resources should be adjusted to meet planned growth. Limitations are defined and recognized by people who work for the company and run it, and who should also accept the fact that they have limitations.

The accounting firm Arthur Andersen disappeared as a result of the ENRON fiasco because someone could not say *no* to dishonesty and give up a lucrative client. The subprime meltdown cost many financial institutions their existence, including the almost-160-year-old Lehman Brothers. RCA, the electronics and music giant, disappeared because it spread itself thin over too many unrelated businesses. Leaders of these companies did not recognize their limitations. Some were blinded by greed, others by ego.

Investments

Companies are limited by the need to balance investments, profits, and cash flow. In spite of being represented in numbers, the decision on such investments is qualitative.

A company that invests in sales or R&D reduces profits while lower investments free up cash but sacrifice the future by not having more sales and new products.

A decision to invest in the expansion of a manufacturing facility is based on a series of assumptions. These assumptions include the future relevance of the manufacturing technology, the sales force's ability to sell most of the added capacity, and the profitability growth needed to support the return on investment. R&D investments are risky because of knowhow gaps, complexity, cutting-edge solutions, end-product costs, barriers to entry, and other start-line factors. There's also risk in predicting the competitiveness or market appeal of a new product or service.

Most product development decisions yield saleable products; yet, often, upon new product introduction, a company finds out that its competition has introduced a similar or better product. In an attempt to regain the lead, management may seek to reduce costs just to find out that the originally chosen platform for the new product does not support cost reduction. Other aspects like too-high manufacturing costs may lead future product lines to be too expensive and require prohibitive rework. Each ingredient might result in an under- or over-investment or lost investment. Other risks may be development of products the market will not buy, or investment in manufacturing facilities whose capacity we cannot exploit.

Research and development is risky, even when "applicative developments" like internet applications, using proven technologies and processes, are concerned. Risks also depend on bringing to market what clients expect, need, or love like features, performance, looks, size, weight, quality and reliability, maintainability, efficiency, and ROI. The risk in R&D, much like in management in general, is that decisions made today will be judged and measured years down the line. Once inside the process, the ability to make quick corrections (in terms of company business cycles) is very low. In some cases, the best option is to courageously admit failure and cut losses. Not an easy move.

Similar dilemmas are relevant to sales, marketing, and finances. Marketing and sales are the face and voice of the company. They are responsible for branding, client relationships, and creating market awareness and consumption of the company offering. Missing a notch in a message, branding, or relationships can be critical.

An important lesson can be learned from Apple Computers. The company prematurely announced the then-new Macintosh computer a few months before Christmas, presenting it as the ultimate Christmas gift, stating its availability before the holiday. As a result, clients put their Apple PC purchases on hold awaiting the new Macintosh. Apple's business suffered a costly slowdown in sales.

When investments are considered, financial management has a key role in securing funds, lines of credit, and cash-flow sanity. A high risk factor in investments is the cost of money in the form of interest rates and installments, penalties and fees, or straightforward dilution of shareholders' holdings.

Let's take a further look at the subprime mortgage crisis. People with low incomes took out loans higher than the value of their assets—their main assets being their houses. Banks *assumed* that housing prices would increase and cover the loan in case of client default. Save-and-loan banks increased their mortgage-funding facilities by raising cash from investors, who received mortgage-secured bonds. Subsequently, the investors decided to back their risk by practically selling their debts to investment funds or institutions that themselves issued bonds to raise the cash they needed to buy the debt and so on. The result is the previously discussed Ponzi pyramid scheme that cost Lehman Brothers its existence and, as stated, could have been avoided.

The Four Company Limbs

Company growth depends on advancing, expanding, and operating its four limbs: Research & Development, Sales & Marketing, Operations, and Finances. Each limb must harmonically support the other three limbs and contribute to company growth—e.g. sales and marketing need to ensure that salespeople sell products that can be delivered by R&D and manufacturing. Manufacturing must support quantities sold by sales, the financial department must provide working capital, and so on.

The product or offering developed by R&D should meet client expectations. The product should be delivered by manufacturing at the required quality, cost, and delivery times, and sales has to ensure clients buy it. Inability to create a harmonic internal discussion between the limbs will result in not meeting all client expectations—including performance, quality, timing, and pricing—and will result in market rejection or problems. Such problems can manifest themselves as product returns, client damages, loss of business, or lawsuits. It is important to know the limits of your organization and focus on your strengths. Shooting too high or too low normally results in failures.

Poor product vision was Apple's problem between 1986 and 1997, when Steve Jobs was absent from the company. During these years, Apple lacked its creative, trend-creating soul. Steve Jobs had the magic touch, the gut feeling of how to create the next teaser for the public to like and follow. This talent was not there during his absence. The new CEO was instructed to focus on efficient operations but lacked the creativity to drive the development of next-generation products. This is an intangible "people limitation." A conscious or unconscious thinking, personality, and creativity issue that exposed the absence of a lead talent. A missing limb.

Volkswagen's 2015 "Dieselgate" crisis, in which the company practically falsified environmental air-pollution tests of its diesel engines, is yet another example. For a company of its standing, this represented a betrayal of public trust. This was a self-made subprime equivalent decision.

Working Capital. Another corporate aspect is working capital—i.e. availability of cash and credit lines used to finance operations until payments are received. Small or distressed companies receiving large purchase orders may not have the financial backing to finance the work unless clients pre-pay.

Let's look at a simple example. A company makes a large sale. To execute it, parts are purchased, units built and delivered. To purchase parts and pay salaries, rent, electricity, shipping, and so on, cash is required. This is the working capital without which delivery and payment collection are not possible. This mundane example is a stumbling block for many businesses.

People. Employees are a key factor, as they have the touch and feel for the product, service, quality, face-to-face client interaction, and so on.

Teams must be able to seamlessly execute their tasks, knowing that financing is in place, execution and service times are realistic, and all resources are available. Management has to isolate its employees from any problems and solve them. Errors result from underestimation of these factors. Even large companies fail sometimes in the estimation of project execution times because of symptoms like:

- Performing headcounts while overlooking talent-counts.
- Lack of realistic leadership.
- Poor management affecting controls, priorities, budgets, and time and effort allocation.
- Lack of detailed planning and identification of critical details: *the devil is in the details.*
- Overestimation of the value of our knowhow base.

Such loopholes lead to delays and latent unemployment, budget overruns, quality problems, rework, and so on.

Understanding corporate qualitative and quantitative weaknesses and leveraging this understanding to support company growth are a success enabler.

Fast Growth

Many companies are lucky to enjoy fast market- or investment-driven growth, but this blessing has its challenges. Fast growth requires a growth-oriented and capable management that understands the challenges it faces and is capable of devising and implementing solutions.

In 1983, in its second year of operation, COMPAQ reached sales of $111M—impressive, for a new company. In an interview, the founding CEO was asked how he'd succeeded in growing the company so quickly. He responded that he'd built the company as a big company from day one. His management team and administrative infrastructures were chosen from day one to serve a large company so that leadership, decision making, infrastructures, and financing were not limiting factors. This enabled him to focus on products and markets and meeting the company's high-level goals.

Growth is limited by three key factors: management, offering, and financing. Good managers choose the right teams, build growth-supporting infrastructures, and drive people to meet company goals.

The theory is easy, but practice is harder. For example, a start-up company with a breakthrough offering starts accelerated growth. Being small, the company employs multi-tasking staff members able to meet goals in the least amount of time, reduce bureaucracies such as documentation, create unclear functional separation, and trust peer goodwill. Growth, in turn, requires a different culture, clear task ownership, more structures, and focused activities.

The transition from small to medium to large corporations represents the boundary problem discussed in Chapter 4. People suitable to lead through initial challenges may not be the right managers to generate consistent growth. Managers of large corporations are not necessarily the ones to run small or startup companies. Thus, each transition between growth phases involves concerns like hiring new people, inventory buildup, sales efforts, time, and learning curves—all of which also represent financial risks. Other risks are success probability, loss of key employees, and use of new technologies.

Awareness is the tool to ensure fast growth. While driving core activities, attention has to be given to supporting functions and financials. Apply awareness through controlling, learning, and improving based on actual results and gaps between results, plans, strategy, and vision. Controls require the implementation of tools to manage cash flow, product performance, output per employee, and so on.

Awareness is an intangible state of mind, a long-term investment continuously used to develop a wide, holistic approach that simplifies management. Awareness is about developing sensitivity to intangibles like identifying weaknesses, building supporting infrastructures, minimizing internal friction, and focusing only on activities that maximize results.

Chapter 14:
Distressed Companies

Distressed companies are all over the place. Some of their executives admit it and some don't; some know and some don't. Some are prey for quick bankers and creditors, but most are victims of poor or incompetent managements.

Turning around distressed companies is a hard, demanding, and lackluster task. Some stakeholders stand on the sidelines, awaiting management failure, while others become unwelcome consultants. Turning around a distressed company requires that a manager transcend him- or herself as a person, leader, and decision maker.

A variety of behaviors lead companies to distress. Stagnation, inability to drive change, not adjusting to changing times, corruption, fear, and generation change in family-run companies are just some. Except for malicious activities, such behaviors drive companies into delay mode. There is a delay in sales, new products, payments, cash flow, and debt repayment. Delays cause instability and chaos, loss of clients, and loss of staff, suppliers, and lines of credit. The challenge is to recognize early enough when internal harmony is lost and to bring the company back on track.

Nevertheless, Charles Darwin's theory of evolution by natural selection is also valid in corporate life: not all distressed companies survive. Prior to reinvesting in distressed companies, one should make an assessment of their survival worthiness and growth potential.

Thrive on Chaos

Rarely are the executives who lead companies into chaos the ones to save them. A new management—or, rather, leadership—is required. This new leadership has to affect employees, clients, suppliers, and shareholders, regaining their trust and backing.

The new leadership's challenge is to make the company thrive in spite of chaos, which is quickly spread throughout the organization's limbs: Sales & Marketing, Offering (products or services) & Technology (research and development), Finances, and Operations. Chaos spills over to clients, suppliers, bankers, and other parties.

Chaos generates symptoms in all company activities, and especially in the people involved. When a company is distressed, so are its people. Walking into such companies, one senses a lack of direction, poor management presence, confusion, reactions, impatience, and unusual levels of gossip, arguments, or loud discussions. Employees try to cross paths with executives and read their eyes, faces, and body language; fewer phones are ringing in the sales department; and phones don't stop ringing in accounting. There are fewer purchase orders, and existing ones cannot be fulfilled as manufacturing slows and inventories are very low or uselessly high.

How then do we generate the change, sail instead of drift, run and not sit, and set our direction when we are at a loss? The key is in leading people. Leading people is a comprehensive statement encompassing a leader and all the people involved, especially the employees. Leading people implies movement, dynamics, and vision.

A leader focuses first on his main working tool: the employees. Talk to them, listen, and do brain mining. Explain what you plan to do. Break the immediate goal or dream into executable tasks. Make sure employees are assigned tasks they can successfully execute. Delegate to free up your time to plan ahead and execute the next stage of "management in motion"—for management is not unlike the military, in which maneuvers must adapt to ever-changing conditions.

In spite of natural defensive, cost-saving instincts, spend the money on visiting clients so you can compile information and show presence—which will be interpreted as strength, existence, and vitality.

Turning companies around is like battling disease. One can fight the symptoms of the disease, or one can work at strengthening the body. A stronger body will fight the symptoms and overcome the disease. Start focusing on daily goals and horizons, gradually expanding to weekly, monthly, and yearly goals. The initial, tedious, seemingly endless effort is crucial. This is where the seeds are sown, the company's state of mind is changed, new standards and work norms are set, and initial results are achieved. Small, personal successes increase motivation, trust, and self-esteem, creating and driving a positive feedback cycle of optimism that generates a new self-fulfilling prophecy.

During the first days and weeks after joining Sememe, I felt employees scrutinizing me. Having seen Sememe's revolving door of executives, managers, and consultants, I knew that I was not being taken seriously. The employees had probably collected bets as to how long "this one" would last. To succeed, I had to pass daily tests. What the team started seeing was my presence, determination, learning, clear decisions, and the chairman's approval or rather lack of his usual intervention. To pass the employees' scrutiny, I focused on prioritizing and synchronizing activities while mentoring executives and steering them to initially achieve their new short-term goals and then the long-term ones. As little successes were achieved, and Sememe's vision became clearer, the positive feedback cycle became self-fulfilling. Motivation, focus, and efficiency became self-drivers.

The chairman cooperated with me, although not always willingly. His cooperation was proportional to his level of despair combined with my determination. I wasn't another yes-man; I did what I believed was right for the child called Sememe.

That's not to say we didn't have rough times. We did. On three occasions the chairman rejected plans for critical activities without which, I thought, the company would not survive. Such activities included the costly but necessary redesign for cost project and giving up the chase after strategic partnerships. I handed in my resignation with the full intent of leaving. It was rejected, I don't know why, and I went on with implementing the proposed plans.

It was fear that drove the chairman's rejection of my plans, fear about the longer-term investment, since he had no idea where the financing would come from (it was financed from increasing sales). My perspective of the same situation was that I could either shut down the company or try to save it by making only the minimum required investments. I opted for the latter.

During that period, current expenses kept piling up and turning into debt, while income was far too low to cover the expenses. I couldn't cut costs quickly enough, and inventories were high. I decided to focus on increasing the top line: sales, creating a long-term impact, and using excess inventories of the old product generation to make and sell products. In parallel, we worked on tactical, one-time cost-cutting measures and initiated development of the new and profitable product line. This required decisive actions targeting the best use of today's time and money to ensure future growth.

Many of the actions involved in managing a turnaround company are mentally and emotionally difficult—from firing people and deciding on new product development to changing the company's direction by tearing it and its employees away from their comfort zones. In such distressed situations, leaders and managers need nerves of steel, some sense of humor, and the right personalities to start moving the corporate mass and get the work done. In parallel, they generate a new vision, however vague, and develop and focus it over time. Last but not least, separate wheat from chaff; prioritize correctly.

Setting Priorities

Priorities are crucial in healthy and definitely in distressed companies. Setting priorities is a skill requiring a holistic view of the goals at hand, an ability to break them down into executable tasks, and a healthy level of investigative willpower. Priority setting also requires managers to withstand pressures like:

- Different client needs that require customization.
- Needing to prioritize long-term growth over an immediate crisis (or vice versa).

- Having fewer funds than the budget requires and therefore needing to prioritize.

- Team members who oppose priorities, reducing their resources or responsibilities.

Distressed companies present the biggest prioritization challenges. They require leadership with the courage to set priorities and implement them under chaotic situations. Under duress, people's horizons narrow, and managers and employees react to immediate events without looking beyond. Under duress, survival instincts pull us to reactive mode—a mode in which priorities are void, resources misused, and time wasted.

Assuming a company is likely to survive, short-term reactive survival should converge with the long-term proactive plan as early as possible. This involves two challenges:

- Deciding on long-term goals (grand and execution strategies)

- Setting implementation priorities (tactical execution)

Determine Grand Strategy and Execution Strategy

The first challenge is to make long-term decisions despite great uncertainty. The results of these decisions will be revealed a few years down the line, maybe sooner. These decisions must integrate a variety of trend-related information such as markets, tastes, and technologies.

Although a reasonable amount of information is essential, it is impossible and impractical to endlessly collect information for analysis purposes, as too many details will delay decisions. Since delays consume much-needed company resources and management attention, quick decisions are needed—which means the courage to decide and implement decisions under duress and uncertainty. As pressures lower, more and more resources will be funneled away from survival and into devising and achieving long-term goals.

Determine Tactical Execution

Our second challenge is implementation. A leader must take his or her team through the *right sequence* of daily steps. Implementation is a leadership challenge in terms of personalities and priorities. It depends on the team—on people. A motivated and willing team of capable *can-do, will-do* people are great partners. Followers will implement plans and reach goals more quickly, efficiently, and effectively than a skeptical team.

Comments such as "But we have been doing this for many years" and "What do you know that we don't know?" are symptoms of stagnation. These symptoms can serve as the basis for analyzing what led the company to where it is. People voicing opinions and taking a clear stance are dialogue partners—contrary to those who make no comments, do not work, or do the wrong work, who pose much bigger risks. This is where leadership comes into play; it is where, in spite of any doubts, the CEO must decide on a clear direction even if future adjustments will be required. Wrongful long-term decisions may cost the company its existence; however, under duress, making decisions is the only way to proceed.

Now that a direction has been chosen and our filters are in place, operational priorities need to be set. The following three interrelated parameters summarize what needs to be prioritized: time, money, and milestones. Setting implementation priorities is a somewhat easier task than formulating strategic decisions, also because these are based mainly on quantitative data.

Managed Crisis: The Shakeup

Distressed companies are victims of their own management—management that instilled, knowingly or not, a certain corporate direction and culture that did not work. Otherwise, the company would not have deteriorated. Under such circumstances, the company— or rather its employees, board of directors, and possibly shareholders—need a shakeup, a wakeup call.

I was called in to help with a company that manufactured composite material products for the construction industry. The company was run around star personalities. The founding star, the techy star, and the sales star were revered. Their personalities and self-perceptions of being almighty in their fields led them to develop a personality cult and promote flexible truth reporting. The majority shareholder was afraid to lose them; nevertheless, he understood that help was needed. After a short learning period, I decided to put knowhow and egos to the test.

First, I probed all the information I was presented with, asking questions, talking with clients and suppliers, and browsing the internet. In doing so, I found many reporting inaccuracies.

Second, I started looking for alternative and proven sources of knowhow.

The stars were shaken. The techy left, the sales guy was fired (trust was the issue), and the founder remained to rebuild a solid and cooperative team. Employees were encouraged to be more open in their communications and

employee and employer in which the worthy employees know they are taken care of.

For many managers, layoffs are the hardest. The moral power to lay off people should be driven by the understanding that if all employees remain on the payroll, the company will collapse, leaving everybody jobless.

Profit vs. Growth

Growth-stage companies need to invest funds to grow revenues. They should use funds for working capital, sales and marketing expansion, development of new products or services, or to increase inventories and manufacturing capacity.

Corporate investments reduce profits, especially if investments are done using company capital. Management's dilemma is how to achieve the balance between increasing profits and risking the future or lowering profits and investing in the future. This issue is especially notable in distressed companies in which small successes become self-fulfilling, activity-accelerating prophecies.

Increasing Sales

In addition to the techniques discussed in Chapter 10, sales may be immediately increased by leveraging existing customer lists, calling upon former resellers, counter intuitively increasing sales travel budgets, focusing marketing messages, providing application information, and stressing technical support and service.

In distressed situations, it is important to focus on personal, one-on-one sales promotion activities. These activities reap valuable benefits.

First, client feedback highlights product advantages, strengths, and weaknesses, and corporate image. Feedback improves sales messages, offerings, features, delivery times, pricing, and service expectations. Verbal discussions reveal cooperative, unhappy, and other client types. People express themselves verbally in a much freer form than in writing. Conversations trigger ideas and comments that provide valuable information.

Second, interpersonal sales activities help identify specific clients with specific needs, sometimes leading to the sale of custom products—creating a new reference and building a basis for future cooperation. Even when no sale is made, one-on-one promotion calls have a marketing and branding impact, making the effort worthwhile.

General marketing activities such as exhibitions, articles, and advertising contribute to branding, image, and market presence but no immediate sales. For cash-hungry distressed companies, the cost effectiveness of these is relatively low because of longer sales cycles. Personal discussions with potential, current, or past clients are cheaper and have greater impact.

A bonus of communicating with clients is employee experience. Representatives need to develop rapport with clients, and struggle to get their attention and business and to serve them. Such personal experiences help transform companies from within, as employees realize—sometimes the hard way—that the real boss is the client. Client off time should be used for planning and preparing further activities and communications.

Sales are strengthened by professional and prompt service and support. Professional, positive support and problem solving give clients and distributors confidence in their business partner. When clients and distributors perceive their partner is strong, proactive, and professional, they're more likely to develop long-term relationships and recommend the company to others.

Remember: hesitation is costly; diligence is essential.

Finances

Regain control by knowing your numbers: the big ones, crucial ones, variables, and fixed expenses.

In addition to operational tools, apply comparative accounting, comparing your financial structure to similar competitors'. Similar structures indicate common successes or common troubles. If your industry has a 40% gross margin, ensure your company has a similar ratio, and so on. If your ratios are negatively different, review them carefully, cross check numbers, validate, and analyze them from different angles in order to develop better understanding of where tuning is required. See which dollar spent provides the highest returns and which one the least return.

If the company's numbers are very different from the industry average, then changes are a must. This is valid for both in-the-red and in-the-blue companies. If the numbers are exceptionally positive (compared to the industry), there is probably an accounting mistake.

Distressed companies suffer from negative cash flow— that is, spending is larger than income. If this is the case with your company, identify expenses that can be delayed, debts to be negotiated, and other financial actions that provide short-term cash relief.

Create a cash flow wellness index to show at a glance your key financial parameters, like projected year-end cash balance or income per employee. These important numbers summarize changes in costs or income. If no material events take place, the magic number remains fixed, indicating a need to continue and push ahead.

Creditors should be prioritized by making a list of debts by importance, first paying life-supporting suppliers. Second-tier suppliers, other creditors, and old or unimportant debts, as large as they may be, should wait. (See the section in Chapter 2 on Finances.)

Initially, cash flow control is more important than profit & loss statements and balance sheets, which are, by definition, historical reports, and quite useless in terms of immediate survival when struggling daily to create a better future.

Preferably, spend cash on small expenses and avoid big or long-term expenses. Push to sell products whose production cycles are shorter, thus reducing the burden on operating cash. Subcontract manufacturing in order to lower overheads and latent unemployment. Negotiate lower interest payments—always a heavy, growing burden. Shift credit lines from banks to suppliers, and reduce operating cash requirements. Differentiate between cash sources for operations and investments, and focus on smaller, financially justified investments while tightly controlling cash drainage.

Further cost savings can be generated across the board by decreasing rent, negotiating better prices, and seeking other sources for raw materials, reducing subcontractors, and financing costs. Cash can be generated by selling off assets, accelerating inventory consumption, and expanding sales.

No matter how little a company tries to spend, working capital and credit lines are indispensable. When negotiating credit lines with banks, provide banks with all the numbers to generate trust and goodwill that can make the difference and turn the tide in spite of bankers' preference to loan umbrellas on sunny days and take them back on rainy ones.

Sememe was deep in the red with banks. Our bankers, feeling uncomfortable with the negative results, decreased credit lines every time a deposit was made. We therefore accelerated sales by consuming inventories and turning them into much-needed cash. I shared with the bank our financials and their improvement. The bank was happy with the results, and our transparency policy developed trust. That trust withstood a sales slump that I knew would translate into a cash deficit two months later. I called the bank manager with our projections and asked him for his support. Trusting us, he tripled our line of credit for a period of three months. We lived up to the expectations and made a timely payback of the loan.

Price Lists

Top management should control price lists, which are the epicenter of the four limbs: Research & Development, Sales & Marketing, Operations, and Finances.

Company price lists are *the* junction between the four company limbs, defining:

- Products and offering for sales and marketing.
- Sales price for clients.
- Delineate what manufacturing should produce.
- Include a reasonable profit.

If the price list does not make business sense or provide the company with a profit, then the numbers or the product strategy should be revised, like raising prices. Will the market tolerate such price rises? Are my products positioned to justify higher prices? Are there enough differentiators to support higher pricing compared to competitors?

In addition, price list information is used in planning activities, which will not be discussed here. The concept is simple, but its implementation is complex due to quicksand aspects such as competition, competitor pricing, market or client expectations, cost of labor, and cost of raw materials. These and other variables converge on our price list—the junction between clients and products and a key component in our budgeting and business plans.

Layoffs

Massive layoffs are synonymous with distress and require careful planning. Hysteria and lack of detailed planning lead managers to fire chief designers or owners of specific relationships or knowhow because they are too expensive. In some cases, this equates to firing the future. Dedicate a few days for a detailed revision of personnel and abilities. Check each and every name, professional contributions, and knowhow while considering the larger picture, future included.

As discussed in Chapter 7, when deciding on who should be laid off, be sensitive and empathetic. All employees have needs, and many have families. Support needy employees by firing those who have better chances in the employment market (age is a factor to consider here). Convey a positive message to employees. Telling your employees what's going on is part of the unwritten trust pact between employee and employer. When the pact is in place, employees work knowing that their backs are covered.

Layoffs should be minimized and done in one round. Staff will be more productive when not threatened by the next round of layoffs. In some cases, to avoid future layoff rounds, you may need to fire more people up front than the immediate deficit dictates.

Layoffs are also part of company policies in order to increase competitiveness and improve employee quality. Some large companies have a policy of firing a certain percentage of their employees every year to contribute to ongoing personnel improvement. In small companies, such policies can be destructive.

Still other companies fire employees whenever salary raises or bonuses are due. Such management is driven by cost savings and the wish to increase profitability and their personal bonuses. This is a poisonous attitude that leads to loss of employee loyalty and higher employee turnaround. Employees seek alternative employment once they understand the pattern.

Over the years, I have been compelled to fire people. My first such experience was as a team leader. It was a case of trust in which my reaction was instantaneous. One day, an engineer working under me did not come to work or leave any message. Worried that something had happened to him, I made a few phone calls, through which I found out that he'd gone to visit friends at his former university. The next day, I asked him about the reason for his uncoordinated absence. He gave me a gross lie. I faced him with his lie, and without consulting my superiors I gave him two weeks' notice and sent him away. Though young, I knew that once lying begins, you never know where it ends.

The second time I fired someone was so hard that I trembled. It was a formative experience for me, a 28-year-old boss. The person I fired was older than I and married with two children. He was a good person but was incapable of fulfilling the position he'd been hired for. He knew it, and I knew it. I identified with him and felt sorry for him. Yet firing him was the right thing to do for both parties, and he accepted the verdict in spite of the humiliation. He was even happy about it and returned to his previous, routine job.

Initiating a Crisis

I was once called upon to lead a change in a relatively small company that had an Eastern European subsidiary. The subsidiary was mismanaged, lost money, and did not deliver its product. Delicately put, it seemed that certain employees were misusing funds. In addition, the local manager, instead of supporting his development team when asked for support, would yell at them. The only way I thought proper to handle this situation was to initiate a crisis, the nature of which was to fire most of the local team. Except for some key employees, whoever wanted to go, I let leave. In some instances, a soft change is neither affordable nor sensible, especially when strategic clients are at risk.

I did the firing as planned. I saw people resign and was left with a group of employees who were clearly unhappy. The remaining employees were unsure what was right for them. One day, as I was about to leave for the airport, a group of employees started talking to me. A younger employee suddenly stepped up and said outright, "We don't trust you!" His timing wasn't perfect, but I couldn't leave such a statement hanging in the air.

I asked him why they didn't trust me, and a dam collapsed. Words started flowing, and I realized that the fired manager had told them that the subsidiary was in trouble because the parent company refused to transfer funds. The former manager obviously forgot to mention his special "arrangement" with the funds. I left with a distressed feeling, strained guts, and sleepless nights.

If the rest of the employees left, we would lose our strategic clients. But we would have also lost them if things had remained as they were. I'd opted for the proactive and riskier crisis-generation process, and it proved to be more rewarding; the reorganization was successful. Messages were clear, communications were open, and the organization started running efficiently.

Operations

Outsource whatever possible. Subcontractors are harder to manage, but they're less trouble and cost in the long run. Subcontractors remove from company financials the responsibility for vacations, insurance, sick days, absence, accidents, machine downtimes, latent unemployment, and so on.

Subcontractors work under specific managers. It's the duty of these managers to get subcontractors to perform to plans, know what to expect (and inform the subcontractors of those expectations), and define how subcontractors will be measured and controlled.

When dealing with subcontractors, don't rely on unwritten expectations. Write down concise definitions of the quality, performance, cost, and delivery times you're agreeing upon and then make sure the subcontractor signs a copy.

A good subcontractor serves as an additional sanity and quality check. Subcontractors, before beginning work on a project, will scrutinize documentation to protect themselves. To ensure no rework is required, they crosscheck all the details relevant to their work. Learning about what subcontractors pay attention to makes your team more sensitive to details they might deem unimportant.

At Sememe, we became very happy with our subcontractors. They were experts in their fields, and they allowed us to concentrate on our expertise: products and markets.

Even when using subcontractors, keep crucial information and experience in your own hands. To protect intellectual property and trade secrets, keep special programming, final product integration, and testing in house.

In short: enhance the company's core competence and farm out the rest.

Qualitative Management

Strategy and tactics can be paired—much like pairing architecture with civil engineering, an artist with a craftsman, or a scientist with an engineer. While the former leads the concepts, philosophy, and high-level goals, the latter converts these into quantifiable and executable tasks. Qualitative directions are high level and descriptive, used as the north star to guide the company, setting the general direction in which the company should advance. The detailed navigation and planning are part of the quantitative planning and execution.

The highest level of qualitative input is the already discussed vision or high-level goal, sometimes wrongfully referred to as the mission statement. Mission statements tend to be more specific, while the company's vision is a generic description of the field in which the company specializes, and it rarely changes. A shift in the mission statement may be illustrated by a book publisher: he may diversify into publishing magazines, but his core competence remains publishing. Similarly, a semiconductor company may add digital devices to its analog product line while remaining a semiconductor manufacturer. An advertising agency may opt to add web-based advertising while remaining in the field of mass communications.

A well-known contrary example is Nokia, established in 1865 as a ground-wood pulp mill that switched to copper cables and rubber and later entered the telecom arena. This process represents a vast shift in the vision.

A company's vision is qualitative. In it, the founders or shareholders of the company decide the company's field of activity. This is a qualitative decision that can be based on anything from gut feelings and opportunity to knowhow. The CEO generates the mission statements, business plans, and resource allocation.

RCA Corporation, once America's pride, placed golden-age radios, records, and record players in every American house. RCA's demise was driven by expansion into other fields like publishing, car rental, frozen foods, carpeting, and greeting cards—fields in which management had no knowledge. RCA's management also invested in new, market-educating, and risky product developments, like the costly and failed videodisc.[14] The management felt their Midas touch would last forever, and so spread thin their attention and financial resources to the point of destruction.

Some companies were led by managements into irrelevancy because of new, disruptive technologies. Their managements were unable to identify trends, to innovate.

---

14 An analog video disc, a predecessor to today's digital video disc (DVD).

Kodak's management failed to embrace their engineer Steven Sasson's first digital camera, developed in 1975, which replaced film and magnetic tape, making Kodak irrelevant.

The transistor replaced the electronic vacuum tube, jet aviation replaced propeller aircraft, and internal combustion engines replaced steam engines—and the Pony Express could not convert itself into a railway company. Natural selection takes its toll.

A simple example of a qualitative-stemming sanity check is the following: an electronics company manufactured a variety of products, each assembled and tested over a pre-calculated number of hours. The total calculated manufacturing hours were 30% lower than the number of actually paid manufacturing hours, indicating the existence of latent unemployment. A detailed analysis revealed one simple manufacturing-floor activity that was understaffed and that therefore became a bottleneck. Newly hired, untrained employees released the bottleneck and *doubled* production output in no time. At this point, all numbers fell into place, lowering per-unit costs.[15] The next qualitative decision was to transfer these cost reductions to distributors, which resulted in more sales and faster inventory turnaround.

---

15 As product output increased, "loaded costs" were reduced.

Conclusion: Looking Ahead

Success is about people: managers, employees, clients, shareholders, bankers, and suppliers. Without *all* these people, a company would lose its reason for existing.

It is up to executives and managers to create success through qualitative and quantitative judgments, leadership, determination, optimism, trust, and creation of positive human dynamics. The morals, habits, and lessons taught by executives will trickle down to employees.

As a manager, it is your duty to:

- Be smart and receptive.
- Be optimistic, honest, and determined.
- Broaden your horizons and form your own opinion.
- Be sensitive, listen, and think out of the box.
- Forget your ego.
- Inspire and lead teamwork.
- Act as you want your employees to act.
- Follow your company's qualitative vision.
- Create qualitative goals and milestones.
- Use sanity checks.
- Say "no" when justified.

As humans, we enjoy our comfort zones and show a certain intolerance to change. Big changes, especially those that we do not initiate and lead, throw us off balance. But change is inevitable; the world is changing in unprecedented geopolitical, leadership, and monetary ways, presenting us with many new opportunities and challenges.

It is up to us to open our minds and hearts to identify changes that will affect our lives.

The principles presented in this book can help leaders make better companies and companies better. It is valid to both healthy or distressed companies and it can be used with any other management tools. Hard and focused work is required because success is not automatic.

The qualitative principles discussed in this book are viable and applicable everywhere: in our personal lives, science, medicine, military, and government and non-profit organizations. While the principles are the same, the environment, context, and language are different.

About the Author

Mr. Jephtah Lorch has decades of experience holding C-level executive positions in Europe and the US. He also led major Homeland Security projects in South America and conducted business worldwide.

At the moment, Mr. Lorch is using his extensive CEO experience to focus on strategy consulting and executive mentoring. He is creating substantial shareholder value by applying his experience and technology background.

Mr. Lorch turned around a bankrupt wireless equipment company, subsequently selling it to a NASDAQ-traded corporation.

He merged a telecom equipment company into a NYSE-traded conglomerate.

He made an exit from an optical company.

He managed several other technology companies.

Mr. Lorch's perspective of management mirrors his people-oriented approach, extensive international and cross-cultural experience, and interest in historical processes. This book provides a conceptual overview of his techniques and field-proven management philosophy.

Made in the USA
Middletown, DE
26 October 2021

51098763R00111